Governance, Compliance, and Supervision in the Capital Markets

Governance, Compliance, and Supervision in the Capital Markets

SARAH SWAMMY
MICHAEL McMASTER

WILEY

For general information on our other products and services or for technical support, please contact our Customer Care Department within the United States at (800) 762–2974, outside the United States at (317) 572–3993, or fax (317) 572–4002.

Wiley publishes in a variety of print and electronic formats and by print-on-demand. Some material included with standard print versions of this book may not be included in e-books or in print-on-demand. If this book refers to media such as a CD or DVD that is not included in the version you purchased, you may download this material at http://booksupport.wiley.com. For more information about Wiley products, visit www.wiley.com.

Library of Congress Cataloging-in-Publication Data is Available

ISBN 978-1-119-38065-8 (Hardcover)
ISBN 978-1-119-38057-3 (ePDF)
ISBN 978-1-119-38064-1 (ePub)

Cover Design: Wiley
Cover Image: © PPAMPicture/Getty Images

Printed in the United States of America.

10 9 8 7 6 5 4 3 2 1

Contents

Preface   vi

Acknowledgments   vii

About the Authors   ix

CHAPTER 1
Capital Markets Participants, Products, and Functions   1

CHAPTER 2
How the Financial Crisis Reshaped the Industry   23

CHAPTER 3
Governance   33

CHAPTER 4
Overview: Capital Markets Compliance   57

CHAPTER 5
Overview: Supervision   89

CHAPTER 6
Central Role of Finance and Operations   99
Ian J. Combs, Esq.

CHAPTER 7
Cyber Risk Role in Governance Model and Compliance Framework   129
Alexander Abramov

About the Companion Website   157

Index   159

Preface

As lifelong practitioners in compliance and governance for the capital markets, we have seen many changes throughout our careers. Some of the changes were driven by the natural evolution of products in the marketplace, but many more by sweeping regulatory reform resulting from the 2008 financial crisis. These changes have obfuscated a clear path to conducting business. We have crafted this book to provide both professionals and nonprofessionals the fundamentals necessary to understand and work through the regulatory frameworks that govern our industry.

Sarah Swammy and Mike McMaster

Acknowledgments

We would like to express our enormous gratitude to our colleagues and friends. As leaders in the industry your experience, technical knowledge, and market insight helped to make this book successful: Alexander Abramov, Ian J. Combs, and John Grocki. Thank you for all of your contributions to this work.

We want to extend a special thanks to Larry Harris and Colin Robinson: Larry for editing the many early drafts of the book and Colin for editing the final drafts.

About the Authors

Sarah Swammy is a senior vice president and chief operating officer for State Street Global Market, LLC, a registered broker-dealer subsidiary of State Street Bank and Trust. She is also a member of the Global Markets Business Risk Committee. Sarah joined State Street from BNY Mellon where she held several leadership positions including business manager and head of supervision for BNY Mellon Capital Markets, LLC and chief administrative officer for BNY Mellon Global Markets and principal overseeing the sales and trading businesses. Sarah has held compliance positions at Deutsche Bank Securities, Inc., CSFB and Barclays Capital, Inc.

Sarah serves as a member of New York Institute of Technology Advisory Board in the School of Management. She is a former member of the Touro College of Education's Graduate Advisory Board and a former member of the Executive Steering Committee for BNY Mellon's Women's Initiative Network.

Sarah holds a BS in Business Administration and an MS in Human Resources Management and Labor Relations from New York Institute of Technology, an MA in Business Education from New York University, and a PhD in Information Studies from C.W. Post. She is also an adjunct instructor at New York University School of Professional Services.

Michael McMaster is a managing director and chief compliance officer for BNY Mellon Capital Markets, LLC, a broker-dealer affiliate of BNY Mellon, chief compliance officer for BNY Mellon's Broker Dealer Services Division, Government Securities Services Corporation, and is also the head of BNY Mellon's Shared Services Compliance Group, which services its broker-dealer affiliates and swap dealer. Prior to joining BNY Mellon in 2010, Mr. McMaster was counsel for Rabobank (a Dutch banking organization), handling securities regulatory matters, and Rabobank's U.S. Medium-Term Note Issuance Programs as well as chief compliance officer for Rabo Securities USA, Inc., the U.S. broker-dealer affiliate of Rabobank. From 1998 to 2002, Mr. McMaster worked for BNY Capital Markets, Inc.—a predecessor entity to BNY Mellon Capital Markets, LLC—and held the position of chief compliance officer. Mr. McMaster also held positions as counsel and chief compliance officer for Libra Securities LLC and was an Assistant District Attorney in the King's County (Brooklyn, NY) District Attorney's Office. Prior to moving into legal and compliance positions, Mr. McMaster was a collateralized mortgage obligation trader for Tucker Anthony. He graduated with an undergraduate degree in Finance from Manhattan College and received his J.D. from New York Law School. Mr. McMaster is an adjunct professor at New York Law School and is chairman of the Compliance Committee for the New York City Bar Association.

ABOUT THE CONTRIBUTORS

After completing his undergraduate studies in business at the State University of New York at Oswego, **Ian J. Combs, Esq.**, moved to New York City. He soon began his career on Wall Street only a few short months before the financial crisis of 2008 by accepting a position with the Financial Industry Regulatory Authority (FINRA). Since then, Ian has worked in several capacities for FINRA, including as an examiner and regulatory liaison as well as holding a position in regulatory policy. During his tenure at FINRA, Ian attended New York Law School in the evening and graduated with honors in 2015. He was also a member of the Law Review and a recipient of the Harlan Scholarship. Ian's primary expertise is in SEC and FINRA financial and operational rules and regulations.

Alexander Abramov is a technology governance, risk, compliance, and information security senior leader with over 20 years of experience in financial services, advisory services, and life sciences. His roles span from the Head of application development, IT audit manager, IT governance and compliance practice leader, to the Head of Information Risk. (www.linkedin.com/in/abramovalexander)

Mr. Abramov has been defining and leading information risk management programs for multiple areas of financial firms, including broker-dealer, swaps dealer, prime broker, proprietary trading, securities finance, collateral management, compliance, and operations. He leads organizations to create risk-based and cost-effective information risk governance frameworks to protect firms' information assets and achieve compliance with applicable regulatory requirements.

Mr. Abramov has been a member of the board of directors of ISACA New York Metropolitan Chapter since 2007, and was elected President in 2017. His credentials include Certified Information Security Auditor (CISA),

Certified in the Governance of Enterprise IT (CGEIT), Certified in Risk and Information Systems Control (CRISC), and FINRA Series 99.

Mr. Abramov is a recognized thought leader in areas of information risk and technology risk governance. He is a co-author of *Cyber Risk* (riskbooks.com/cyber-risk), published in London in 2016. An accomplished speaker, Mr. Abramov has presented at over 30 conferences in North America and Europe on the topics of risk management and IT compliance.

CHAPTER 1

Capital Markets Participants, Products, and Functions

This chapter provides an introduction to the participants, products, and functions of capital. We also discuss the important role capital markets play in supporting economic growth and development (Figure 1.1). We start with a detailed discussion of key participants and how capital markets support their economic activities. We then introduce the foundational product groups offered and review their key features and uses. Then we will explain the various types of markets and how they facilitate the funding and investing needs of participants.

THE BASIC PRODUCTS OFFERED IN CAPITAL MARKETS

For the focus of our discussion we view capital markets as offering two types of funding products to issuers: Equities and debt (also called fixed income) through both primary (initial issuance of securities) and secondary (ongoing trading of securities) markets. From a broader perspective, capital markets may also include the trading commodities, currencies, and derivatives.

Equities

Equities, also known as shares and stocks, represent an ownership interest in a corporation; the term *share* means each security is a share of ownership in a corporation. Shares have the same limited-liability rights of the corporations they represent, which means that the liability of share owners is limited to their investment amount. Shares are initially created when a corporation is formed, whereby the owners can choose the number of shares appropriate for the corporation's plans and valuation. At this point the corporation is known as a private corporation, as all the shares are held by a close group of investors.

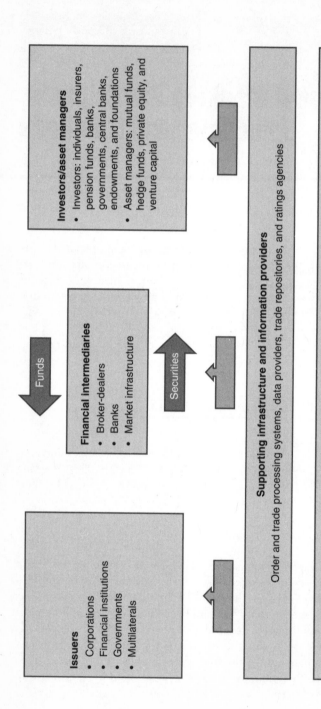

Issuers
- Corporations
- Financial institutions
- Governments
- Multilaterals

Financial intermediaries
- Broker-dealers
- Banks
- Market infrastructure

Funds

Securities

Investors/asset managers
- Investors: individuals, insurers, pension funds, banks, governments, central banks, endowments, and foundations
- Asset managers: mutual funds, hedge funds, private equity, and venture capital

Supporting infrastructure and information providers
Order and trade processing systems, data providers, trade repositories, and ratings agencies

Market enablers
Regulation and legislation: Corporate governance and investor protection, accounting and reporting standards, securities regulation, and industry regulation
Social and macroeconomic policies: Pension/retirement policies, tax regimes, and education (financial)

FIGURE 1.1 Capital markets environment.

As corporations grow, some may choose to become a public corporation, or one that is listed on a public stock exchange, where members of the public can openly buy or sell shares. This process is known as listing where existing or additional shares may be created and offered to the public through an initial public offering (IPO).

Shares entitle their holders to a share of the dividends declared by the firm's board of directors to be distributed from the corporation's profits. Likewise, they also generally entitle owners to a vote on critical decisions at annual general meetings. Shares can be created in different classes with differing rights. There are two broad classes of shares, common and preferred. Preferred shares typically have a higher claim on dividends and on the assets of a firm in the event of liquidation, but typically have no voting rights and have a fixed dividend that will not rise with earnings.

Following an IPO, shares are traded on stock exchanges and their valuation is subject to supply and demand, which in turn is influenced by the underlying fundamentals of the business, macroeconomic factors such as interest rates, and market sentiment.

The return to shareholders is a function of both the dividends paid to them from the corporation's profits and of any movements in the share price (capital growth). Importantly, too, equities have the lowest rights in the default and liquidation of a corporation and are the last to be paid out.

Fixed Income

Fixed-income securities, as the name suggests, promise a fixed return to investors. Fixed-income funding is similar in nature to the provision of a loan by a bank, but issuers manage to attract a broader investor base through tapping into capital markets, generally lowering the required interest rate or improving non-price terms for the borrower.

Fixed-income securities typically have a maturity date when the security expires and the principal or loan amount is paid back to the investor. Most fixed-income securities also offer interest rate payments (known as coupons) at regular intervals. Some types of securities, such as zero-coupon bonds, do not pay out any coupons while inflation-indexed (also called inflation-linked) bonds index the principal amount to inflation and floating-rate bonds offer a variable interest rate based on a benchmark market (variable) interest rate plus a premium.

There are two broad types of bonds based on the issuer: Corporate bonds are issued by corporations, and sovereign bonds are issued by governments. A third type includes municipal bonds issued by governments at the subnational level, which are particularly common in the United States. Sovereign securities are also referred to as rates, as the main risk is related to movements in market interest rates. This is based on the assumption that the sovereign is risk free—an assumption that has sometimes proven false as we have seen 30 sovereign defaults from 1997 to 2014 alone.[1] Corporate bonds are also known as credit securities, as the primary risk related to these is the underlying credit risk of the issuer.

Fixed-income securities are also tradable in the market and are thus subject to market price movements. Given that the interest rate payments are largely fixed, any decline in interest rates raises the effective yield of the security (coupon payment as a percentage of value of the security). As a result, there would be increased demand for the security, driving its price higher and reducing its yield. Thus, the prices of fixed-income securities typically move inversely to movements in interest rates. Furthermore, a change in sentiment about the credit quality of an issuer can result in a decline in the value of those securities.

Foreign Exchange and Commodities

Foreign exchange (FX) relates to the trading of currencies in exchange for other currencies. The most basic form of FX transaction is a spot trade where two currencies are agreed to be exchanged immediately at an agreed rate. FX is frequently broken down into G10 (comprising the 10 largest developed countries) and EM (currencies of all other countries).

Commodities represent basic goods, typically used in production and commerce. There are many types of commodities traded, with each commodity represented for contract purposes using a variety of sizes and qualities based on historical conventions. When commodities are traded on an exchange, they must conform to strict quality criteria to ensure standardization of each unit. The key groups of commodities include, but are not limited to, agricultural, animal products, energy, precious metals, and base metals. Commodities are largely traded in the form of derivatives contracts.

Derivatives

Securities can be classed also as cash and derivatives. Cash securities represent direct ownership or claims on assets, such as part of a corporation or a financial obligation from an issuer. Deriv, as the name suggests, derive their value from an underlying asset such as other securities, indices, commodities, or currencies (FX).

Derivatives typically represent future claims on assets, for example, if a commodity is bought for future delivery via a forward contract. Hence, they are heavily used for hedging purposes by a wide variety of market participants. Hedging involves offsetting some form of risk, such as potential future changes in interest rates or the potential change in the price of a commodity. When used as a hedging tool, derivatives effectively transfer the risk in the underlying asset to a different party. As such, derivatives can also be thought of as providing a form of insurance. The most common types of derivatives are *forwards, futures, options,* and *swaps*:

■ **Forwards:** Forwards represent binding contracts for the sale or purchase of a fixed quantity of an asset at a fixed point of time in the future. Forwards are most commonly used in the FX and commodities markets.

■ **Futures:** Futures are similar to forwards except that their contract terms are standardized and they are traded on exchanges. Futures are also available on many index products including stock indices.

■ **Options:** Options, as the name suggests, provide the right (but not obligation) for the contract holder to either buy (known as a call option) or sell (put option) a certain fixed quantity of an asset either before or at a fixed expiry date at a fixed price. Options can help provide a floor price for certain assets (i.e., through owning a put option, which guarantees a certain sale price) or a ceiling price (i.e., through a call option, which guarantees a maximum purchase price) for certain assets, thus minimizing risks faced by the option holder.

■ **Swaps:** Swaps are contracts by which two parties agree on the swapping or exchange of two assets or commitments at some point in time. The most common form of swaps is interest rate swaps (IRSs). These contracts swap the interest rate payment commitments between two counterparties. The two main types of IRSs include float for fixed, where a floating interest rate commitment is swapped for a fixed interest rate commitment, and float for float, involving the swapping of a floating rate based on one benchmark rate with another. Both involve fixed notional or principal amounts upon which the rates are calculated.

CAPITAL MARKETS AS A SUBSTITUTE FOR BANK LENDING

We described the narrow definition of capital markets as the provision of funding to issuers. In that sense, capital markets serve similar functions to traditional banking. Banks facilitate the provision of funds to customers to support their economic activities. Banks traditionally raise their own funding through customer deposits and thus match investors supplying funds with issuers requiring funds. They also help transform the maturity or term profile required by each of these parties, with investors typically seeking to part with their funds mostly for short periods, and issuers looking for longer-term funds.

Banks traditionally relied on their deposits for a significant proportion of their lending; thus deposits were the primary limit on lending. However, now, under most modern fractional reserve banking systems (which we will not detail here), banks have the unique ability to also create money. To highly simplify the process, when a bank creates a loan (an asset on its balance sheet), it simultaneously also creates a deposit in the loan customer's account (a liability on its balance sheet). The deposit is effectively new money, created by the bank, which the customer can then utilize. This is known as the money creation effect. Banks could theoretically offer unlimited lending and create unlimited new money; however, they face several regulatory restrictions on their activities. These regulations result in banks having to optimize between several constraints to their lending and deposit-taking activities based on the quality and quantity of loans, deposits, other funding, and capital (can largely be thought of as shareholders' equity and reserves). In effect, the deposit base and capital position of a bank serve as key restrictions on overall lending growth. The main regulations have converged globally around the Basel accords and local requirements. At a high level, these regulations are:

- **Leverage ratio:** Constrains the ability of a bank to leverage its balance sheet, thus representing a constraint on lending in relation to capital. The leverage ratio is defined as a bank's highest quality capital (Tier 1 capital) divided by its exposures (on-balance-sheet exposures, derivatives exposures, securities financing exposures, and off-balance-sheet exposures). Basel 3 sets the leverage ratio at 3%.

- **Liquidity coverage ratio:** Requires banks to hold an amount of highly liquid assets (e.g., cash and government bonds) generally equal to 30 days of net cash flow. This requirement helps ensure that banks can meet any immediate cash shortages through the sale of their liquid assets. Liquid assets generally do not include lending, and so this requirement also restricts lendable assets.

- **Capital adequacy ratio:** Sets a minimum capital requirement based on a bank's risk-weighted assets. Riskier lending and assets generate higher capital requirements. This requirement also further constrains the amount of lending banks can engage in based on their capital.

- **Loan-to-deposit ratio:** In many emerging markets, lending is also directly constrained by the size of deposits based on the loan-to-deposit ratio. In Indonesia, Bank Indonesia, the central bank, enforces a maximum loan-to-funding ratio of 94% at the time of this writing. Here, funding includes demand deposits, time deposits, medium-term notes, floating rate notes, and bonds that are issued by banks.

Given the constraints faced by banks, capital markets offer an important alternative source of funding for issuers and alternative investment options for investors. From an issuer perspective, fixed-income securities allow a broader range of funding options compared to bank loans. They are highly customizable and allow for a broader investor base, enabling issuers to raise funds that banks may not be willing to provide in the form of a loan given constraints discussed earlier. Of course, capital markets also offer the option of raising equity funding, which is not available generally from banks. From an investor perspective, both fixed-income securities and deposits offer a fixed return. However, fixed-income securities allow investors to take corporate credit risk, create a more diversified portfolio, and access different points on the risk/return profile, whereas deposits, which tend to be at least partially insured, typically offer the lowest return for investors.

THE KEY STAKEHOLDERS IN CAPITAL MARKETS

There are four primary stakeholders in capital markets:

1. Issuers (principally corporations, financial institutions, government, and multilateral organizations) that seek funding for business activities
2. Investors who seek a financial return on their investment and/or seek liquidity
3. Financial intermediaries that ensure an efficient flow of money from investors to issuers
4. Supporting infrastructure and information providers that sustain capital markets by providing critical information to market participants

Issuers

Issuers represent the demand for funding in capital markets and seek to obtain funding for a variety of reasons, differing based on the type of issuer. In general, issuers seek funds to develop or maintain economic projects that generate cash flow. The cash flow from these projects is partly used to pay for the cost of funding obtained. There are four main categories of issuers: Financial corporations, nonfinancial corporations, sovereigns/governments, and quasi-sovereigns or international multilateral organizations.

Overall, corporations are by far the largest issuers in the capital markets, and we differentiate here between financial and nonfinancial corporations as their needs and use of funds, along with the types of funds used, can differ considerably. Each of the issuers is discussed in more detail here, and the types of capital markets products they use will be covered in the next section.

Corporations (Nonfinancial Institutions) Nonfinancial corporations include both public (listed) and private unlisted firms. These firms require funds for carrying out their various economic activities with funding requirements typically differentiated between the term required:

- **Long-term capital:** Longer-term investments include the construction of factories, purchasing or developing equipment, acquiring other firms, and funding research and development—typically investments that generate cash flows that span beyond one year. Specific funding products can include term loans (from banks) and/or a combination of equity funding and fixed-income bonds.
- **Short-term capital:** Typically classed as working capital and used for purchasing of items and inputs to production that are expected to be sold within one year. Working capital is typically funded either through short-term working capital loans, overdraft facilities, and credit cards provided by banks and other financial institutions or through short-term capital markets products such as commercial paper.

Financial Corporations From an issuer perspective, financial corporations include banks, thrifts (also known as savings and loans in the United States), building societies, and credit unions, but also to a lesser extent investment managers such as fund managers. Financial corporations are also significant users of capital markets and are highly involved as intermediaries, too. While many of them have investment needs as corporations (e.g., for branches or IT systems), we highlight two distinct funding purposes:

1. **Asset-liability management (ALM):** ALM is the process of managing structural mismatches between assets and liabilities on the balance sheet. In a bank, these include the balancing of lending and/or investments (assets) and deposits and other non-equity funding (liabilities). ALM is also a vital function of financial institutions such as insurers and asset managers, which have significant maturity transformation roles or frequently changing assets and liabilities. Mismatches arise and change on an intraday basis due to the changing profile of assets and liabilities and market movements. Capital markets are utilized to manage and balance these mismatches as they occur.

2. **Investment leverage:** Some investment managers such as hedge funds will utilize capital markets for generating leverage on their investments—essentially raising funding from capital markets in the form of debt, enabling them to invest more than the sum of their investors' funds with the aim to generate higher leveraged returns.

Sovereigns/Governments Sovereigns and governments (used interchangeably) are also significant users of capital markets in most economies globally although smaller in aggregate than corporates. In larger economies such as the United States, governments at all levels, including the federal/national, state/province, and local/municipal level, are active users of capital markets while in smaller economies, typically only the national and state governments are in a position to seek funding through capital markets. Governments typically require funding from capital markets for two broad uses:

1. **Non-capital expenditure:** In many cases, government expenditure on consumption items that directly provide goods and services to their population (i.e., health care, education) exceeds general government income including but not limited to personal and business taxation, duties, fees, and asset sales. In this situation, the government's budget is said to be in deficit. Governments typically need to borrow funds from capital markets to fund this gap and ensure essential public services can be provided.

2. **Capital and infrastructure project development:** Governments are also primarily responsible for providing infrastructure such as highways, airports, hospitals, and schools. These, too, may require borrowing funds from capital markets if funds cannot be provided from general government income. Some of these projects may generate ongoing revenue streams in the future, which will assist in covering their borrowing costs.

A third but related point is that during times of economic stress (recessions), governments often use fiscal measures such as increasing public spending with the aim of creating extra demand and stimulating economic growth to lift their economies out of recession.

Government securities are typically issued by their treasury departments. However, certain sizable government entities that engage in significant financial activities may also seek funding on their own. These include, for example, the Federal National Mortgage Association (FNMA) or "Fannie Mae," a publicly traded corporation that is a government-sponsored entity (GSE) and supports the national mortgage market.

Investors and Asset Owners

Investors, or asset owners, represent the supply of funding in capital markets and seek to obtain a return for supplying funds to issuers. Investor assets vary widely, with advanced economies having significant investment funds and emerging and developing economies much smaller pools of funds.

Investors can be any individual or institution in possession of funds and seeking to generate a return from those funds. The key categories of investors are discussed in the following.

Individuals Individuals have a variety of options for generating returns from their savings. Usually the largest investment made by individuals is their home. Individuals may choose to keep any extra savings funds in bank accounts, although these typically yield lower on average than other options. As a result, individuals increasingly participate in capital markets, either directly as in the purchase of equities or bonds through a broker, or indirectly through placing their funds with an asset manager.

With the prevalence of online brokers, and the diversification of their offerings, retail investors can now directly participate in many capital markets products. Retail capital markets activity is largely concentrated in equities because of ease of use, low fees, and typically less complex products. Retail investors can easily trade ETFs and basic derivatives such as stock options and contracts for difference (CFDs) while in some markets fixed-income securities are also easily accessible through brokers.

Insurers Insurers collect premiums from their policyholders and use these proceeds to invest in assets that will eventually support the payment of claims according to insured life events (death, terminal or critical injury, etc.), property and casualty events (fire, injury, etc.), and health events (hospitalization, medical care, etc.) by their claimholders.

Pension Funds Pension funds aggregate the retirement savings of individuals. For pensions managed and provided directly by employers, the pension fund represents the employer's contributions to meet their future pension obligations to their employees. Individuals and/or their employers make regular contributions to these funds, usually as a proportion of monthly pay, and this is invested to grow over their working life. Given their size in some countries, pensions represent a powerful class of investors. Upon retirement, individuals either withdraw their pension for usage or convert their pension fund into an annuity that pays regular cash flows. In an increasing number of nations, contributions to pensions are mandated, including Australia (Superannuation), UK (Workplace Pensions), and Singapore (Central Provident Fund), to mention just a few. Governments have realized that as the share of the working-age population declines and as people live longer, the government is less able to fund extensive social security programs and that individuals will need to be responsible for retirement income. As such, pensions represent a sizable share of available funds and are very important given the millions of individuals who rely on them for retirement income and for saving governments from extensive social security payments. Pensions originally were largely structured as a defined benefit where investors were guaranteed a fixed benefit or payment based on their incomes or regular contribution amounts. Given fluctuations in asset prices and difficulty in forecasting, together with the fact that life expectancy has increased significantly in the past 50 years, pensions are increasingly adopting a defined contribution structure, where the benefit is dependent on both contributions and the investment performance of the pension.

Banks Banks invest in capital markets products as part of their asset–liability management (ALM) process. However, banks need to be prepared for any short-term shortages in liquidity and thus are required to hold a significant amount of highly liquid assets (set to be at least 100% of net stressed cash flows over a 30-day period under the Basel Liquidity Coverage Ratio rules). This should ensure that in the event of a liquidity crisis, banks can convert these assets into cash in capital markets relatively quickly to cover cash shortfalls.

Governments Governments can generate surplus funds, either through budget surpluses, through asset sales (national firms, commodities, etc.), or through foreign exchange surpluses. Many governments have created state funds tasked with investing these funds, known as sovereign wealth funds (SWFs). The investment of these funds is extremely important given that their income supports national budgets and national investment in infrastructure and facilities such as schools and hospitals. Given the size of these funds, they must tap capital markets to source appropriately sized investments.

Central Banks Following the financial crisis of 2008, central banks have become significant investors in capital markets through the use of quantitative easing (QE). QE involves the purchase of securities (largely government securities) from banks to reduce yields and enable banks to increase lending activity with the additional funds in order to stimulate economic growth. The United States (Federal Reserve), Europe (European Central Bank), and Japan (Bank of Japan) have all extensively used QE over the past decade to stimulate economic activity.

Central banks also participate widely in capital markets as part of their role to implement monetary policy and in some cases as part of their role in managing exchange rates. In many countries, central banks manage the key overnight reference interest rates through trading activity in overnight repo markets, effectively setting the rates banks lend to each other overnight. Repos (repurchase agreements) are short-term collateralized loans made between two parties where one party borrows money in return for securities and agrees to buy back the securities at a fixed time. Repos are vital instruments for short-term financing in many capital markets.

Endowments and Private Foundations Endowments are trusts made up of funds, usually donated, and dedicated to provide ongoing support for the activities of certain institutions. The most well-known endowments include those established to support universities or charitable not-for-profit organizations. Endowments invest their funds through capital markets and supply a portion of the investment returns to support their beneficiary institution, occasionally also utilizing some of the funds when investment incomes may be low.

Investors/asset owners may directly manage their capital markets investment decisions or place their funds with asset managers who make investment decisions for asset owners based on various investment strategies. Asset managers either offer segregated and bespoke mandates to institutional investors or aggregate investible funds from numerous investors into funds, each with clearly defined investment policies and principles.

There are four types of basic fund structures:

1. **Mutual funds:** Mutual funds typically issue units, each representing a proportion of the total fund, allowing investors to purchase an investment in the fund based on their desired size. Mutual funds can be structured as closed-ended or open-ended. Closed-ended funds issue a fixed number of units when a fund is launched. They are normally listed on a stock exchange, and investors are only able to enter and exit by buying and selling existing units in the fund, with units priced by the market. Closed-ended funds commonly utilize leverage in their investments. Open-ended funds do not have a fixed number of units and thus can accept new investments (through the creation of new units) or redemptions (through reducing the number of units) based on demand for investing in the fund.

2. **Hedge funds:** Hedge funds seek to generate a positive return in all market conditions. As a result, hedge funds will often have complex investment strategies, utilizing a broad variety of investment products spanning many asset classes, including significant usage of derivatives. In contrast to mutual funds they face fewer investment restrictions.

3. **Private equity funds:** Private equity (PE) funds make medium- to long-term equity investments in both listed and unlisted corporations. Typically, the PE fund's aim is to take an active role in managing the firm and to fix issues and improve the firm's profitability. Typically, PE firms will aim to achieve a controlling stake in an investment where they seek to significantly influence management. Once performance is improved, PE funds aim

to offload their investments, either through a sale to another firm, or through an IPO at a higher valuation, generating superior returns.

4. **Venture capital funds:** Venture capital (VC) funds also largely make equity investments. While similar to PE investments in many ways, venture capital is provided at a much earlier stage than typical private equity investments, usually to promising start-up businesses with little or no revenues; thus there is a high degree of risk associated with venture investing.

Financial Intermediaries

Financial intermediaries enable capital markets to operate across the full breadth of products, facilitating the matching of the specific needs of investors and issuers. The main categories of intermediaries in capital markets are: banks (investment banks), broker-dealers, exchanges and clearing organizations, central securities depositories, and custodians. Apart from banks and broker-dealers, these intermediaries are also known as market infrastructure.

Banks (Investment Banks) We've already discussed the function of banks as investors and issuers. Banks also play two further significant functions in capital markets. These include the investment banking function (discussed here) and the broker-dealer function (discussed in the next section).

The investment banking function supports firms to raise funding from capital markets and to also broker mergers and acquisitions deals between firms. There are three broad subfunctions within investment banking:

1. **Equity capital markets (ECM):** The ECM division of an investment bank is responsible for supporting issuers to raise funds through the issue of equities to the public. ECM teams are usually specialized by industry to enable them to effectively determine the value of the issuing firm and its securities. ECM divisions also maintain large networks of potential investors to support the distribution of the securities. ECM teams also support firms in ongoing equity capital raisings, through rights issues, for example. As part of the ECM function, investment banks often underwrite the securities, or agree to buy a pre-agreed level of the securities if they fail to attract sufficient interest from investors.

2. **Debt capital markets (DCM):** The DCM division supports issuers to raise debt financing for corporate and government issuers. Similar to ECM teams, they are often specialized to ensure they can accurately determine the right structure and pricing for debt issuances based on the unique characteristics of the issuer and the prevailing market conditions. In certain markets, some of the largest dealers are also denoted, typically by the Department of

Treasury, as primary dealers. These dealers represent the only dealers that may directly transact with the Treasury department or national central bank in government securities. Typically only the largest and most well-managed dealers are allowed this privilege.

3. Mergers and acquisitions (M&A): M&A teams support clients in merging with or acquiring other firms, and also divesting parts of their business. While not directly a capital markets activity, M&A transactions often require significant financing and often collaborate with ECM and DCM teams.

Broker-Dealers   Broking (brokering) and dealing are two separate functions, although they are often discussed together given that their core functions are complementary and often offered in an integrated manner. Brokering essentially involves the execution of capital market transactions without taking on any risk. It is also called acting on an agency basis when dealing in equities and riskless principal when dealing in the fixed-income markets. In essence, brokers connect two parties to a transaction, either through a trading medium such as an exchange, or directly as in over-the-counter transactions. For this service they charge a commission.

Dealers, in contrast, act on a principal basis, willing to use their own balance sheet to make a market for clients (known as market-making). Dealers quote a spread for each security they are willing to trade in. The spread refers to the difference in the price they would be willing to buy or sell a security at. Dealers thus may have to sometimes serve as the counterparty to a trade until a further counterparty is found. Banks can now largely only undertake such principal transactions for their clients under the Volcker Rule in the United States and its equivalents elsewhere. These rules prevent banks from putting their own capital at risk in high-risk, short-term trading transactions that are not directly related to benefiting their clients (known as proprietary trading) to increase profits.

A subset of brokers are inter-deal-brokers, who only look to serve broker-dealers themselves as their clients.

Broker-dealers also provide advice to their clients on which investments to make, often supported by teams of research analysts. The research reports of broker-dealers are highly important in supporting investor participation through the dissemination of trade ideas while also keeping a close check on the performance of issuers. Research has generally been bundled into brokers' trading commissions and thus not charged for separately, although recent reforms under Europe's MiFID II have seen research unbundled and charged for separately to minimize potential conflicts of interest and increase transparency for end investors.

Exchanges, Clearinghouses, and Central Counterparties (CCPs) Exchanges are venues where buyers and sellers of securities meet to transact/trade in those securities. Today, most exchanges, particularly for equities, are almost completely virtual; however, some still maintain trading floors where traders representing the brokers of buyers and sellers physically meet and agree to trades. Historically exchanges specialized in certain asset classes, the most well-known of which are stock exchanges where equities are traded. Other key exchanges include commodities exchanges such as the Chicago Mercantile Exchange (CME). Increasingly, exchanges have been diversifying over the past decade, with credit fixed-income products, exchange-traded funds, and a host of derivatives offered on exchanges.

Following the execution of a trade, there are two key post-trade processes conducted: Clearing and settlement. In the United States, all equities are cleared through the Depository Trust and Clearing Corporation (DTCC) group centrally, while multiple clearinghouses exist for other securities and derivatives, including CME Clearing and ICE Clear.

Clearinghouses assume the role of intermediary between buyers and sellers of financial instruments. They take the opposite position of each side of a trade, which helps to minimize some netting exposure, thus improving the efficiency of the markets, and adds stability to the financial system. Netting refers to the process of consolidating multiple trades into a single trade, resulting in each partly only having to make a single transaction based on the net value of multiple transactions. The benefits from netting alone can be very large, substantially affecting the economics of a trade.

Central Securities Depositories Central securities depositories (CSDs) are registrars responsible for maintaining the original ownership records for securities and facilitating the settlement and transfer of securities between owners. Traditionally, securities were issued on paper with the owners' names registered and stored in large safes by the owners. Trading was complex with certificates having to be physically delivered. As trading volumes increased, storage of the certificates was first centralized and then digitized, and today almost all securities globally are stored in electronic databases maintained by CSDs. Transfers of securities are now done through electronic book-entry, that is, changing the ownership of securities electronically without moving physical documents.

Custodians Custodians are banks responsible for holding assets such as capital markets securities on behalf of investors. In their safe-keeping or custody role, custodians ensure that the assets of clients managed by large investment firms are held safely and accurately in their names. In their asset-servicing role, custodians also support the clearing process, corporate actions processing (such as dividends and stock splits), and also assist with transaction accounting and reporting. Typically, investment fund assets and collateral for trades are safeguarded by a third party so that they are separated from the assets of the investment manager protecting the underlying investors and are transacted within the bounds of their various investment mandates. There are two types of custodians:

- **Global custodians** safeguard assets for their clients in multiple jurisdictions around the world and are generally the first level through which institutional investors and broker-dealers engage in the clearing and settlement process. Global custodians maintain accounts at multiple local CSDs and/or sub-custodians, covering most geographical markets, or link to local sub-custodians. Global custodians also offer several value-added services, including the optimization of client collateral, collateral processing, and reporting.
- **Sub-custodians** offer similar services to global custodians except that they are typically limited to one or a few local markets. They thus can facilitate access to local markets to clients using global custodians, which have limited local presence. Market participants could connect to sub-custodians either directly or through global custodians with their role being protected by local regulations. Sub-custodians also provide more customized local services, including the handling of localized withholding taxes.

Supporting Infrastructure and Information Providers

Several other important institutions also exist that support the smooth operation of the capital markets. Some of these institutions include:

- **Order and trade processing system providers:** These systems support market participants in making and then managing trade orders. They also support the processing of the trade order, including matching orders between the buy- and sell-side, completing order information, and confirming settlement details to settle and complete the trade. Given the complexity and volumes of trades, particularly in over-the-counter (OTC) markets where trading is highly customized, these systems are essential. A host of firms offer varying solutions, with most solutions offering highly specialized services catering to one part of the trade value chain for certain participants and for a subset of securities. There has been a trend for broadening of solutions across the value chain in recent years and hence some consolidation as participants seek to minimize complexity.
- **Data providers:** Significant volumes of data are required for markets to operate efficiently and effectively. Numerous data providers exist and

support data requirements across the full value chain of capital markets from client onboarding and due diligence, to economic and market research, to trade price discovery and portfolio management. Several providers exist, often specializing based on the types of markets and securities covered. Some of the most well-known names include Bloomberg, Standard & Poor's Capital IQ, and Thomson Reuters.

■ **Trade repositories:** OTC markets have traditionally been highly opaque given the lack of a central exchange. Given that trades can also take days to settle and the frequency of trading, tracing the true final owners of securities can be complex as securities change hands. An example was during the 2008 financial crisis when large defaults such as that of Lehman Brothers highlighted that often the total outstanding values of OTC positions were difficult to estimate and that all counterparties were also difficult to immediately identify. Trade repositories were introduced to centralize the collection and reporting of trade data. Trade repositories store information on all outstanding OTC trades with reporting increasingly mandated globally, allowing regulators and counterparties to have clear, verified, and comprehensive information.

■ **Ratings agencies:** Ratings agencies assess the risk of a default on borrowings (credit risk) of borrowers. These agencies play a vital role in capital markets, assisting investors with guidance on the risk that an issuer may default. Ratings are primarily expressed as a grade based on the probability of default, and while primarily applied to debt markets, are also very helpful for equity markets. Ratings are applied at the issuer level (i.e., corporations) and can also be generated for individual debt securities based on the structure and terms and class of the security. Issuers pay close attention to their credit rating as the costs of borrowing are closely related to their rating, and also as some investors may only be permitted to invest in rated and more favorably rated securities (e.g., investment grade).

TYPES OF MARKETS

Primary and Secondary Markets

Primary markets refer to the initial issuance of equity and debt securities, where the securities are newly created (or originated) and then issued to the market for subscription. The processes for issuance of equities, credit, and government securities were discussed earlier.

Following the initial creation of the securities, subscriptions, and their listing, the ongoing trading of securities on exchanges is referred to as the secondary market. The primary and secondary markets can be seen as substitutes in some ways, as investors can choose to invest in newly created securities or buy existing traded securities. However, each security type can differ considerably.

Secondary market volumes drastically exceed primary markets as they represent the ongoing trading of securities over time for equities. This also holds for many classes of bonds although many bonds are usually held to maturity. Both primary and secondary market volumes can fluctuate significantly. Primary market issuance in equities, for example, is highest when economic conditions are best and when issuing companies can demand a higher price. Primary equity markets can sometimes virtually shut down when economic times are challenging. Secondary market volumes, both for equities and fixed income, can also change drastically during periods of economic uncertainty when market participants are changing their expectations and making significant shifts to their portfolios.

Exchange and Over-the-Counter (OTC) Markets

Exchange markets are those where securities are traded over an exchange serving as an intermediary to match buyers and sellers of securities. These include stock, futures, commodities, and other products. Exchanges provide real-time data on the demand and supply for each listed security in their order books, which display the volume of each security type available for sale/purchase and the corresponding prices asked/offered. Trades are made when there are matching prices from buyers and sellers. Securities listed on exchanges are standardized in that there are generally only a few classes of securities for each issuer. Given the level of standardization, securities transactions are typically settled electronically within three days of the trade and bid, and offer prices are visible and published; thus there is a high degree of price transparency.

OTC markets refer to the trading of securities or contracts through a dealer network as opposed to on a centralized exchange. OTC contracts are typically highly customized (non-standardized) and there is a broad array of securities available within each asset class. The most common types of OTC-traded securities are fixed-incomes securities, non-exchange traded equity securities and certain OTC derivatives on securities.

A single listed corporation, for example, may have fixed-income instruments issued, each issued at a different time, for a differing term, with a differing face value and coupon payment. As a result, liquidity is more dispersed and less suitable to a central order book approach.

Derivatives can trade on an exchange—like equity options or future—or can trade in the OTC markets. Typically, customized derivatives trade in the OTC markets. Given the high degree of customization, varied liquidity, and large trade sizes in OTC markets, pricing can have wider bid-offer spreads and rely on complex formulas together with significant judgment.

Given the high degrees of customization and involvement of significant manual effort in the execution of OTC transactions, trades can typically take longer to settle. Significant amounts of manual verification work are required for trades to be processed, including for the details of counterparties to be exchanged, for trade contract details to be verified, for payments to be processed, and for the trade to be recorded.

One factor that exacerbated the effects of the 2008 financial crisis was that, facing default, several banks and other market participants struggled to identify the final counterparties to many of their OTC derivatives transactions and struggled to settle outstanding trades. This led to the virtual freezing of market trading activity, increasing risk to all participants. A key pillar of reform efforts since the crisis has focused on increasing automation of trade processing, mandatory clearing (through a central counterparty), improved (and increasingly mandated) trade recording, and the centralization of trade, counterparty, and settlement details. As an example, the bulk of interest rates and credit default swaps are now traded on Swap Execution Facilities (SEFs) and centrally cleared with regulations introducing penalties for uncleared swaps in the form of increased and/or mandatory exchange of margin. While exchange trading is virtually electronic at this time, OTC trading is becoming increasingly standardized and electronic to reduce risks and to increase speed and accuracy.

Dark pools are another category of markets. Dark pools are a type of alternative trading system (ATS). Dark pools are a type of exchange where traders can buy and sell securities privately without revealing their identities and without revealing transactions to the public. Dark pool trading has increased significantly in recent years, rising to over 30% of trading by some estimates in the United States. Supporters of dark pools argue that they allow for larger trades without disrupting regular markets, and improve liquidity for larger orders. Conversely, opponents of dark pools argue that they reduce transparency and reduce liquidity, thus leading to pricing impairments.

CAPITAL MARKETS DEVELOPMENT

As discussed throughout this chapter, capital markets can provide an important source of funding for several types of issuers, thus supporting their economic activities and growth. Capital markets can provide a diverse range of investment opportunities, helping investors achieve increased portfolio diversification.

This section provides a brief overview of the drivers of capital markets development through a recent work completed by Oliver Wyman and the World Economic Forum on capital markets development.

In sum, capital markets development rests on three pillars:

1. The breadth and depth of investment opportunities available (issuer side): This refers to the level of participation in capital markets by issuers and the extent to which they utilize capital markets versus other forms of funding (e.g., bank loans, private funding, and retained earnings). The broader the issuer base (across types of issuers, types of projects, variety of industries, levels of maturity) the broader the range of investment opportunities in the market. Advanced markets like the United States provide a wide range of such opportunities. Individual investors, for example, can choose to invest in almost any sector through the stock market and in firms with varying levels of maturity. They can also invest in a variety of government debt (largely through fund managers), and also in infrastructure projects through a variety of methods.

2. The breadth and depth of the investor base: This addresses the range of investors available to provide funds to issuers through capital markets and the size of investible assets. As discussed earlier, investors have a broad range of preferences across risk, return, term, cash flow, and so on. The broader the investor base, and the larger the availability of funds to invest, the larger the range of investment opportunities that can be supported.

3. The strength of supporting market infrastructure, regulations, and supervision: Effective capital markets require a strong regulatory and legal framework given the complexity of products and their economic significance. These frameworks guide standards around disclosure, issuance criteria, and investment manager duties, for example. They are vital for building trust across the numerous participants and standards to understand the products available with consistency. Furthermore, they facilitate the development of strong, reliable market infrastructure, including stock exchanges and other trading venues, ratings agencies, and data sharing.

REGULATORY AND SUPERVISORY FRAMEWORK

Needless to say, a strong regulatory and supervisory framework with clear, fair, and prudent standards for governing capital markets is fundamental. As discussed earlier, capital markets involve a multitude of supporting infrastructure, from exchanges to ratings agencies, from data providers to custodians. Trust is a fundamental characteristic and ensuring the stability and robustness of each of these institutions, together with ensuring the highest standards of their work, is fundamental for strong capital markets. As mentioned earlier, even the most advanced economies are still continuing to refine their capital markets frameworks. This process is unlikely to pause as markets, their products, and their participants evolve. The details of governance, regulation, and supervision will be covered in subsequent chapters.

NOTE

1. Moody's "Sovereign Default and Recovery Rates, 1983–2013," April 11, 2014.

CHAPTER 2

How the Financial Crisis Reshaped the Industry

Capital markets have changed fundamentally following the 2008 financial crisis. In this chapter we discuss the transition from the pre-crisis period, when investment banks experienced record profit levels, to the world we observe today. We discuss the main measures that the regulators introduced following the crisis and their impact on investment banking business models. We conclude with thoughts on the effects of these changes on the functioning of capital markets.

THE SITUATION PRIOR TO THE FINANCIAL CRISIS

Sales and trading in fixed-income and equity instruments and primary market investment banking activities enjoyed a period of tremendous growth from 2000 to 2007. Industry revenues almost doubled to $300 billion over this period. This compares to global GDP, which rose 60% in nominal terms over the same period. Investment banks posted record profits and advertised high targets for shareholder returns on equity.

This strong industry growth had several drivers. Benign economic conditions and strong economic growth in most global regions accelerated asset accumulation and drove up investor appetite for risk assets. Liberalization of banking structures and of national financial systems meant that banks could benefit from a wider array of funding sources and compete in a wider range of markets, leading many to acquire smaller rivals along the way. Financial innovations, such as the invention and adoption of new kinds of derivatives and structured products, and the increased use of leverage when running capital markets operations, enhanced the financial toolkit that banks could deploy to generate revenues.

Banks also managed financial resources in a simpler way than today. Most banks primarily focused on generating revenues and converting leverage into profit. Banks generally managed to "economic capital" as the firm's scarce resource, measuring capital needed using internal statistical models that captured various drivers of risk and resource consumption. Minimum capital requirements imposed by regulators were rarely binding (for example, the expectations of banks' investors as to what Tier 1 capital ratio to maintain were often more stringent than the regulatory minimum ratios), and liquidity was readily accessible in the markets. The use of capital, leverage, liquidity, or funding was sometimes allocated internally for the purposes of performance measurement and resource prioritization, but the respective trading desks had to cope with relatively few constraints.

Regulatory constraints were not as stringent as today. For example, there was little in the way of monitoring or capitalization of derivative positions, or meaningful restraints on the amount of total leverage that wholesale banks could deploy. Because of this, banks allocated financial and operational resources to those businesses earning the highest return on economic capital—as a result, growth in structured derivatives, securitization, prime brokerage, and structured credit all accelerated. Equally, a looser standard of governance existed in the back office, with derivatives collateralization often less than complete, and over-the-counter derivatives had significant settlement backlogs.

In this way, the wholesale banking industry's growth in revenues and profits was driven as much by the relatively permissive regulatory environment and looser financial resource management as by the macroeconomic and market conditions.

OVERVIEW OF REGULATIONS INTRODUCED 2008–2015

The global financial crisis had many causes and expressed the weaknesses of the financial system in many different ways. Both stand-alone broker models and global banks sustained heavy losses and either went bankrupt, sold themselves to competitors, or needed public bailouts. However, it was largely the stand-alone investment bank models that ceased operations altogether as the universal bank models benefited from diversification—although these banks, too, sustained very heavy losses in a few cases. Example of weaknesses within the wholesale banks that were identified by regulators included:

- Hidden leverage in the system built up through the use of derivatives, which were largely treated as off-balance-sheet exposures and were often not fully capitalized
- Insufficiently sensitive and often underestimated market risk capital charges for traded capital markets products

- A lack of robust liquidity and funding risk frameworks at banks, with an overreliance on short-term funding backing up often less-liquid assets
- While still small in absolute terms, a growing reliance on proprietary trading and/or principal risk taking to boost profit generation within the context of banking structures often funded partially through retail deposits
- Insufficient compliance and governance controls frameworks, leading to several large scandals

To tackle these weaknesses, global and national financial regulators introduced a number of regulatory reforms, the bulk of which were accounted for at the global level by Basel 2.5 and Basel 3, in the United States by the Dodd-Frank Act, and in Europe MAR (Market Abuse Regime), SMR (Senior Manager Regime) by regulatory reforms such MiFID as well as various country-led initiatives. While the cumulative weight of regulatory reforms runs to several thousand pages, the principal ambitions from the regulators can be summarized as:

- Increasing the amount and quality of capital that banks (especially banks deemed systemically important) use to back their assets
- Restricting leverage in banks' balance sheets, that is, the ratio of debt to equity
- Improving the liquidity positions of banks, that is, the ability to meet their liabilities as they come due
- Ensuring more stable funding (i.e., promoting a longer-term funding structure with less reliance on short-term wholesale funding)
- Limiting risk-taking, in particular preventing banks with retail deposits from taking proprietary trading risks
- Upgrading governance standards, enabling a fundamental change in bank governance and the way boards interact with both management and regulators

These ambitions were expressed in various new post-crisis rules and approaches. Some prominent examples include:

- Higher standards of capitalization ratios, expressed by core equity and Tier 1 ratios, that is, the amount of capital a bank needs to hold for a given amount of risk-weighted assets. Basel 3, one of the cornerstones of post-crisis global financial regulation, forced up minimum total capital ratios to an 8% minimum total capital ratio, plus a 2.5% capital conservation buffer. For many global banks this was a significant hike in the amount and capital—but also in the quality of capital, as previously there had been a large amount of hybrid capital and other capital types allowed to count toward banks' capital, versus the newer approach of a much tighter definition of *core* capital, that is, primarily tangible common equity.

- Introduction of additional capital buffers for the most complex banks. As part of the authorities' stated desire to tackle the issue of "too big to fail" in the wake of the crisis, after rescues of financial institutions and failures of complex organizations, new rules also forced the most complex financial institutions to hold additional capital buffers of up to 2.5% of RWA (on top of the capital conservation buffer).

- As well as needing to hold more capital for a given level of RWA, risk weightings for assets also increased. The set of regulations known as Basel 2.5 increased market-risk-weighted assets. Within Basel 3, new charges for counterparty credit risk were introduced. More recently, newer rules such as the Fundamental Review of the Trading Book and the move to a *standardized approach* for risk-weighted assets caused further increases in the amount of capital banks must use.

- As a complementary measure to the risk capital ratios, Basel 3 introduced the leverage ratio, which was intended to be a measure of total exposures regardless of risk profile. The Basel 3 leverage calculations brought much of previously off-balance-sheet activity into the capitalized perimeter. Although many market participants expected the leverage ratio to be intended to be a backstop to the risk capital requirements, the introduction of the leverage ratio has turned out to be a major focus for banks with large capital markets operations, in many cases necessitating wide-scale optimization programs and putting pressures on balance sheet and inventory.

- Because several of the large stress events of the financial crisis were liquidity related, regulators introduced the *liquidity coverage ratio* (LCR). It requires banks to hold an amount of highly liquid assets (e.g., cash and government bonds) generally equal to 30 days of net cash outflow. This requirement is supposed to ensure that banks can meet any immediate cash shortages through the sale of liquid assets. Liquid assets generally do not include lending, and so this requirement also restricts lendable assets. In the current interest rate environment this has led to a situation where the cost of funding can be higher than the yield on these liquid assets.

- The Volcker Rule in the United States pushed to restrict proprietary trading activity and oriented the industry toward a more client-activity-focused, revenue-generation model.

- In derivatives, the whole infrastructure of trading was overhauled. Dodd-Frank in the United States and MiFID in the EU mandated much of the market for simpler derivatives to be executed electronically on exchanges or so-called swap execution facilities (SEFs), and cleared through a CCP.

- Regulators combined many of the new measures mentioned earlier into consolidated stress tests, which require banks to hold adequate levels of capital and liquidity to survive simulated periods of severe market volatility. The Fed's CCAR program in the United States has become a major focus point for all large financial institutions.

Many of these regulations were intended to be implemented globally with consistent standards. However, due to the inconsistent application of regulations across jurisdictions, the regulatory landscape has become more patchwork and hence increased the complexity of operating international investment banks. It also led to the occasional accusations of an uneven playing field between banks of different jurisdictions.

IMPACTS ON BUSINESS MODELS

The regulatory reform landscape, in combination with stagnant GDP in many markets, has started to significantly impact business models. It has affected the industry's revenue-earning capacity, it has led to a significant increase in costs of operations, and we are starting to see an impact on competition and concentration levels in the industry. We explore these three trends in this section:

1. Reduced revenue-earning capacity
2. Increased cost of operations
3. Changing competitive landscape

Reduced Revenue-Earning Capacity

The year 2009 marked a high point in industry revenue generation from a historical viewpoint. In this year, massive rebounds in asset positions from the previous nadirs of the year before were coupled with a partial return of positive investor sentiment following authorities' interventions, supercharging market flows. Many banks had hoped for a fast and sustained recovery and had started to set higher targets on growth mode again. Total wholesale banking revenues exceeded $315 billion in 2009, yet by 2015 industry revenues had fallen away 30% to $220 billion. Over the same period, global GDP grew in nominal terms by 30%.

Accounting precisely for the fall in revenue generation is challenging, but the decline is driven at least in part by four factors: More stringent regulation pushing the sell-side (investment banks) to reduce their presence, a particular set of macroeconomic conditions discouraging institutional and corporate clients from risk taking or hedging, a general downward pressure on margins in dealing in sales and trading products, and a fall in risk appetite by the management of investment banks. Things have been aggravated by a so-far-unmaterialized hope for a last-man-standing advantage, resulting in banks retaining business with subpar economics for too long.

For example, the introduction of the leverage ratio has lessened returns in balance sheet–intensive businesses such as repo (repo and reverse-repo financing outstanding by US government securities' primary dealers has fallen from $6.5 trillion to $4.0 trillion between 2008 and 2015). Higher counterparty risk charges have dented returns in structured derivatives where several banks have downsized or ceased operating.

However, the decline in industry revenues is by far not only driven by the change in the regulatory environment; it has also had macroeconomic drivers. For instance, the post-crisis period was characterized by central banks injecting liquidity into the financial markets on an unprecedented scale, which collapsed interest rates and dampened volatility in asset prices for several years. A prolonged period of ultra-low interest rates has been supportive for economic growth and for certain wholesale business lines such as debt capital markets. However, for most other business lines the low-volatility, low-spread environment has dented wholesale banking returns by limiting institutional clients' interest in participating in the markets. For instance, the relatively flat shape of yield curves has dampened demand for hedging products while the decrease in credit spreads over the same period has lessened the incentive for investors to take on relative value trades.

More, margins that the investment banks have been able to generate in making markets in equity and fixed-income and investment banking products have declined in many products. One reason for this is transparency. The move to push standardized derivatives onto swap execution facilities shifted derivatives from historically being bilaterally negotiated between dealers and clients toward looking more like exchange-traded instruments, and clients were able to achieve tighter pricing as a result in many instances.

Another reason is electronification. Improvements in trading technology have encouraged a higher percentage of assets to be traded electronically, although at different rates of growth for different asset classes, and this has also aided new types of non-bank competitors to break into the market-making business, pressuring the average margin per trade that banks could hope to extract. This has been particularly pronounced in FX, where so-called multi-dealer platforms now hold more than 35% of the market.

Understandably, the period between 2009 and 2015 has also been marked by a noticeable increase in bank shareholder risk aversion, with post-Lehman equity holders in wholesale banks no longer willing to risk the bankruptcy of the banking group for the sake of potential short-term profits. Banks have themselves acted to enhance risk management standards, to strengthen the capital base through both equity and hybrid capital, to more tightly limit trading desks' use of capital, funding, and liquidity, and to more tightly monitor and limit value-at-risk for trading activities. While this risk aversion aims to make the banking group safer, tighter risk limits also constrain the ability of trading desks to benefit from arbitrage or risk-taking opportunities.

Increased Cost of Operations

As a result of the regulatory reform agenda, banks now need to manage their business against a varied set of financial constraints.

In a world of restrictive regulatory constraints, pursuing activity in one area generally means forgoing activity in another area. This creates a comparative advantage that can be used to pursue new opportunities. For example, an investment banking business with an outsized repo financing book may be up against the leverage-based capital constraint, but consumes relatively low levels of RWA (risk-based capital) or liquidity and funding. This will generate capacity to pursue more RWA-consumptive business (e.g., structured) or more liquidity- and funding-consumptive business (e.g., mortgages) with a relative pricing advantage over risk-based capital or liquidity- and funding-constrained competitors, all else equal. Moreover, risk–return comparisons are extremely sensitive to changes in interest rates, which makes it even more difficult to draw strategic conclusions.

Against this backdrop, investment banks' strategy setting is increasingly encompassing both franchise- and resource-driven decisions. Franchise-driven decision making has always been a feature of strategic planning—identifying and prioritizing the "crown jewels" of the franchise where the business enjoys genuine competitive advantages, be they client types, product groups/structures, or geographies. Multidimensional resource-driven decision making is the new frontier, requiring a deeper understanding of how the pursuit of crown jewels creates advantages or disadvantages in the pursuit of other opportunities (and ultimately drives economics).

Banks are responding to this challenge in different ways. Almost all have been upgrading their internal information environment, so that calculations on how much different clients and products are consuming across risk capital, liquidity, and balance sheet can be produced quicker, more accurately, and at a more granular level. Most banks have re-educated their front office such that salespeople, traders, and originators are now cognizant of the financial resource implications of positions they are about to create.

As a result of this, we have seen the cost of operating these businesses going up. Banks have significantly invested in their risk management and compliance capabilities. With the future regulatory landscape now clearer, but with new regulations on the way, firms are looking to rationalize their technology worlds—again with post-crisis regulation the driving force.

Changing Competitive Landscape

The shape of investment banks' participation in the markets is evolving in two ways: The banks are becoming more selective in their product and client portfolios, and non-banks are picking up some of the value chain.

Due to new regulatory and market pressures, banks have taken a harder look at their own areas of excellence and areas where they lag peers in service provision, and this is increasing the dispersion in competitive models. Whereas in the pre-crisis period, many banks had similar business models leveraging similar strengths, this is no longer true. Looking at the top 20 financial institutions active in sales and trading and investment banking, many different models are observable. Some are corporate-focused models, typically leveraging strong fixed-income capabilities such as rates and FX, looking into adjacencies in transaction banking (e.g., payments cash management, trade finance) to provide a more comprehensive offering to their CFO and corporate treasurer clients. Some are focused on serving institutional investors, primarily with equities capabilities, whereas others are more wealth-focused, catering to the needs of (ultra)-high-net-worth clients in combination with asset and wealth management arms. Others again are specialists in emerging markets assets and service models with depth in certain geographies and emerging markets products.

THE IMPACT ON CAPITAL MARKETS FUNCTIONS

The forces of change imposed on investment banks have also had a broader impact in the securities industry as a whole. There has been a clear shift in value capture. Since 2006 sell-side revenues have fallen by 20%, whereas buy-side revenues have risen 45% and market infrastructure has stayed flat. Banks cutting capacity and de-risking is an important factor. But the macroeconomic climate has also supported this shift as quantitative easing has translated into strong asset growth benefiting asset managers.

Low volatility and weak economic recovery continue to depress sell-side revenues. Revenue capture by market infrastructure providers—including custodians, execution venues, clearinghouses, and data providers—is broadly flat, albeit with significant shifts within this group, mainly toward the tech and data providers.

Risks have also been shifting. The sell-side is continuing to de-risk across the board while risks in the market infrastructure (MI) layer have grown with the introduction of central clearing and initial margins.

The biggest shift has been toward the asset owners. While liquidity provision by banks is falling, assets under management (AuM) in daily redeemable funds has grown rapidly, up 76% since 2008, with more than 45% of all globally managed assets now sitting in daily redeemable funds, up by three percentage points since 2008, with increased investment in less liquid asset classes (e.g., high-yield credit). With the continued growth of defined contribution (DC), an even larger share of total industry assets sits in retail-related funds, although DC structures such as 401(k) plans in the United States are stickier since investors can only switch funds rather than redeem outright.

Yet in this new environment, execution conditions have also changed, particularly in cash bond markets. Here, the principal focus lies with liquidity, that is, the ease with which clients can buy and sell securities with limited market impact within a given time period.

Credit trading is a key focus point today, with the prospect of rising US rates adding an additional amount of urgency to the debate. A confluence of a significant surge in primary issuance since the crisis, a strong growth in mutual fund holdings with daily liquidity, and markedly lower dealer inventory levels combine to prompt many market participants to fear a liquidity-related market dislocation in credit. Debt issuance has grown at a 10% CAGR globally since 2005; primary issuance in 2014 was 2.4 times 2005 levels. Mutual funds offering daily liquidity have more than doubled their holdings of US credit since 2005 and now hold 21% of outstanding securities globally, compared to 11% in 2005. And dealer balance sheet in corporate credit is down 30% globally since 2010, and we expect another 5 to 15% to come out.

The ultra-low interest rate environment pushed investors toward higher-yielding assets, creating strong demand for corporate credit, while issuers have looked to take advantage of attractive financing terms and to move away from pressured bank lending. The pressures come from a number of sources:

- Most directly, capital and funding costs on dealer inventories have increased four to five times.

- Many also cite concerns around proprietary trading limits (e.g., Volcker Rule) and earnings volatility as another constraint on risk appetite.
- Many market participants feel that increased requirements on transparency (such as TRACE in the United States) have made providing liquidity through market making more challenging (for example, by recycling risk back into the market in the given "transparency window" once a position has been taken).
- Some also feel that increased buy-side concentration in credit and the growth of passive strategies (e.g., trackers, ETFs) have contributed to an environment of more correlated flows, often occurring at the same time (fixed-income ETFs have grown 27% per annum since 2008).

The concern is that while holdings of corporate bonds have materially shifted toward mutual fund structures that offer daily liquidity to their investors, the liquidity of the underlying assets has significantly reduced—although there is actually considerable debate about whether market liquidity has actually reduced so far or whether the impact would only be materially felt in a period of market stress.

On one hand, improvements in financial technology have enabled the proliferation of electronic sales, which has enabled faster and easier trading for clients at a lower cost than the older voice models. Electronic trading platforms have also introduced new trading protocols, which have benefited market liquidity by increasing the pool of potential participants.

On the other hand, the regulatory reforms have driven banks to decrease the total size of trading inventory in products such as investment-grade and high-yield bonds, where banks were the traditional matchers of buyers and sellers of bonds. Moreover, electronic trading and new marketplaces will grow—but will not solve the fundamental concerns.

As with much in finance, there are not many easy solutions to the liquidity conundrum as policymakers face an unresolved conflict among regulators' desires to reduce the riskiness and interconnectedness between banks, to ensure that asset managers have sufficient liquidity to deliver on promises to their investors, and to preserve companies' flexibility to issue in a wide range of markets and tenors. Yet resolution of this conundrum is critical to ensure capital markets remain effective channels of funding to support the global recovery.

CHAPTER 3

Governance

The sophistication and complexity of financial companies and the products and services they transact in, the interconnected nature of their structures both with other parts of their domestic economy and globally, underpin the emphasis on effective management and oversight of these institutions. The regulatory reforms enacted as a result of the 2008–2009 financial crisis emphasize, and in many instances codify, that a board of directors has overall responsibility for a regulated financial entity such as a bank, broker-dealer, swap dealer, or other financial company and that these responsibilities and duties should include approving and overseeing the implementation of the enterprise strategic objectives, governance framework, and corporate culture. The board is also responsible for providing oversight of senior management both strategically and operationally. In essence, in the post-reform world in the United States and in those countries with developed financial markets, the board owns both what goes right and what goes wrong in the company to a greater and more granular extent than in the past.

We will focus on the role and governance of the institution of and by the board of directors as they have ultimate responsibility for the company's business strategy and financial integrity, safety and soundness, key personnel decisions, internal organization, governance policies, structure and practices, as well as responsibility for the critical functions of risk management and compliance. The board has a duty to its various constituencies, including depositors or clients, shareholders, and regulators to practice diligent oversight. This includes clearly defining key responsibilities and authorities of the board itself, of senior management, and of those responsible for executing the control functions such as compliance and risk. The members of the board should exercise their duties to the institution under applicable laws and regulations and be mindful of conventions and guidelines. This includes actively engaging in the major matters of the company and keeping up with material changes in the business and the external environment as well as acting in a timely manner to protect the long-term interests of the company.

Within this framework the board of directors should:

- Establish and monitor the company's business objectives and strategy.
- Define and implement the corporate culture and values.
- Implement an organizationally appropriate governance structure.
- Develop, along with senior management and the control functions of the company, the risk appetite of the enterprise. This should take into account the competitive and regulatory landscape, the long-term objectives and interests of stakeholders, risks that accompany the product or service offered, and the ability to effectively manage those risks.[1]
- Monitor compliance with its stated risk appetite, related risk policies, and limits:
  - For banks, broker-dealers, and other financial institutions, approve and oversee the implementation of the capital adequacy process, capital and liquidity plans, compliance policies, and system of internal controls.
- Approve the selection and oversee the performance of senior management; and in the case of many types of entities subject to regulatory reform, including banks and swap dealers, oversee the design and operation of the compensation system and monitor and review the system to ensure that it is aligned with the stated culture and risk appetite of the company.

In addition, the board should oversee transactions with related parties (including transactions between and among an affiliated group and with those entities that might be deemed affiliates by regulation or convention), so that transactions are reviewed to assess the risks involved and are subject to appropriate limitations. Inter-affiliate transactions involving a depository institution, such as a bank, and a non-bank affiliate are subject to specific regulation in the United States under Federal Reserve Board Regulation W, as well as in the UK, the European Union, and a number of other jurisdictions.

The board of directors should review periodically the governance framework so that it remains appropriate in the light of material changes in the business's size, complexity, geographic reach, business strategy, regulatory requirements, case law on entity or corporate governance, and relevant best practices.

Post–2008–2009 financial crisis regulatory reforms and, preceding that, the U.S. Corporate Sentencing Guidelines during the 1990s recognize that a basic component of good governance is a demonstrated corporate culture of reinforcing appropriate norms for responsible and ethical conduct.

These norms are critical to an institution's risk awareness, risk-taking, risk management, and ability to respond to inappropriate conduct. In order to promote a sound culture for the institution, the board should take the lead in establishing the "tone at the top" by:

- Setting and following corporate values, both for itself as well as senior management and other employees, to create expectations that all business should be conducted in a legal, transparent, and ethical manner.
- Promoting risk awareness within a strong risk culture, conveying its expectation that it does not support inconsistent risk-taking, and communicating that all employees are responsible for helping ensure that the company operates within its stated risk appetite and risk limits.
- Actively communicating the corporate values and standards or codes of conduct it sets for itself, all levels of management, and employees and increasingly those the company may do business with.

Equally substantive is the process for ensuring that all employees, not just senior management, are aware of the consequences for violating these policies as well as the practical aspects of how to report and escalate violations and the rights and protections they enjoy, commonly referred to as whistleblower protections. As this norm and companion regulatory requirement matures, many company codes of conduct or codes of ethics, or comparable policies, are defining in very specific detail what constitutes acceptable and unacceptable behavior. As a baseline, standards, policies, and codes should expressly forbid actions that could lead to regulatory or reputation risks or improper or illegal activity such as financial misreporting, money laundering, fraud, anticompetitive practices, bribery and corruption, or the violation of consumer or privacy rights. The issue of confidentiality and freedom from reprisal are themselves becoming increasingly robust areas of focus and enforcement by governmental and regulatory agencies.[2]

Banking and other financial regulators increasingly expect that there should be direct or indirect communications to the board (for example, through an independent audit or compliance process to a committee of independent directors or through a third party/ombudsman independent of the internal "chain of command"). The board should also make a hands-on determination as to how and by whom apparently legitimate matters should be investigated and addressed by an identifiable, objective, independent internal or external entity, senior management, and/or by the independent directors or full board itself.

GOVERNANCE, OVERSIGHT, AND CONTROL

It might be stating the obvious, but it is important to note that financial companies take risk: Market risk, credit risk, and many others. Regardless of whether the company takes risk into its inventory, intermediates the risk, or tries to hedge out the risk, it is important to know and understand what business you are in. The board of directors plays a key role in this regard because it is responsible for oversight of an appropriate risk governance framework. The effective risk governance framework in a financial institution includes a strong risk culture, a well-developed risk appetite framework communicated through the risk appetite statement, and well-defined responsibilities for control functions such as risk management. Constructing and communicating the institution's risk appetite in a documented and unambiguous way is essential to reinforcing a strong risk culture. The board should clearly define and communicate actions to be taken when stated risk limits are breached, including disciplinary actions for inconsistent or excessive risk-taking, the related escalation procedures, and the manner in which the board will be notified of any matters.[3]

The board should take an active role in developing the risk appetite and ensuring its alignment with the company's strategic, capital, and financial plans and compensation practices. The company's risk appetite should be clearly conveyed through a risk appetite statement that is easily understood by all relevant parties: the board itself, senior management, employees, and regulators.

The institution's risk appetite statement should:

- Frame risk in both quantitative and qualitative decision criteria.
- Clearly define risk, using readily available or observable measures, the individual and aggregate level, and types of risk that the institution is willing to assume in advance of and in order to undertake its business transactions within its risk capacity.
- Clearly outline the parameters and business decision criteria under which the institution is expected to operate when executing its business strategy.
- Actively communicate and socialize the board's risk appetite throughout the institution, linking it to daily operational decision making and establishing the channels to communicate and escalate risk and strategic issues across the company.

While risk appetite development may be initiated by senior management, an effective risk appetite statement needs both top-down board leadership and bottom-up management involvement at all levels of the organization. To make it work successfully, rather than be merely another piece of paper, requires meaningful communication among the board, senior management, financial and risk management, as well as operating managers across the businesses.

A risk governance framework should include well-defined organizational responsibilities for risk management and compliance functions, typically referred to as the three lines of defense:

1. The line of business or identifiable business unit (commonly known as the first line of defense)
2. Risk management and compliance functions independent from the business (the second line of defense)
3. An internal audit function independent from the first and second lines of defense. (The Basel Committee on Banking Supervision Principles for Sound Operational Risk Management and the COSO: Committee of Sponsoring Organizations of the Treadway Commission Internal Control Integrated Framework outlines the needs for and structure of an independent internal audit function.)

Depending on the institution's nature, size, and complexity, and the risk profile of its activities, the specifics of how these three lines of defense are structured can and should vary. With that distinction in mind, the structure and responsibilities for each line of defense should be well defined, documented, and effectively communicated.

Business units, sometimes referred to as the front office, the first line of defense, whatever they might be called, own the risk to the organization. They take transactional, product, and aggregate risks and are responsible and accountable for the continuing management of such risks. This includes identifying, assessing, and reporting exposures and related measures and mapping activities to the organization's risk appetite, policies, procedures, and controls. The way in which the business line executes its responsibilities should reflect the company's business model and structure.

The second line of defense includes an independent and effective risk management function. This function complements the business line's risk activities by executing its monitoring and reporting responsibilities. Among other things, it is responsible for overseeing the institution's risk-taking activities and assessing risks and issues independent of the line of business. This function should promote the importance of senior management and business line managers in identifying and assessing risks critically rather than relying only on surveillance conducted by the risk management function. (Some organizations, as a top-down matter of governance, have a narrowly defined authority embedded in the risk function to supersede first-line decisions.)

The second line of defense also includes an independent and effective compliance function. This function should, among other things, routinely monitor compliance with laws, rules, and regulations to which the institution is subject. The board should approve compliance policies across the organization and actively communicate them to all staff. The compliance function is responsible for supporting the development and execution of policies and reporting to senior management and, as needed, to the board on how the enterprise is managing its compliance risk. The compliance function should be independent and also have sufficient authority and stature within the organizational hierarchy, appropriate resources, and access.

The third line of defense consists of an independent and effective internal audit function. Among other things, it provides independent review and assurance on the quality and effectiveness of the institution's risk governance framework, including how it translates into organizational culture as well as business strategy planning, compensation, and management decision-making processes. Internal auditors must be appropriately trained and professionally competent as well as have no conflict of interest to the extent that they are not involved in developing, implementing, or operating risk functions or controls, which could, as a matter of optics, be viewed as compromising their independence.

The board should own the positioning of the risk management, compliance, and audit functions in the organizational hierarchy and see to it that they are appropriately staffed and resourced and carry out their responsibilities independently and effectively. As part of its oversight of risk governance the board should regularly review policies and controls with senior management and with the heads of the risk management, compliance, and audit functions to identify and address significant risks and issues, as well as determine areas that need improvement. Whether this should be a push or pull process as part of board meeting administration is dependent upon the corporate secretarial function and where it is positioned in the organization.

Oversight of Senior Management

Failures of corporate governance over the past 30 years, both high-profile examples such as Enron, WorldCom, or Lehman Brothers as well as more routine examples, highlight the importance of having a board actively involved in selecting the CEO and potentially other key members of senior management, as well as increasingly the heads of the control functions as well.

The board should provide active, regular, documented oversight of senior management. Obvious though it might seem, the board should ask questions, thoughtful questions, something that was conspicuously absent in the record of many notorious corporate and governance failures. The board should hold members of senior management accountable for their actions and communicate the consequences if those actions don't align with the board's performance expectations. The board is responsible for overseeing senior management's adherence to the company's values, risk appetite, and risk culture. In doing so, the board should:

- Oversee senior management's actions for consistency with the business strategy and policies approved by the board, including, prominently for banks, the risk appetite statement.
- Establish dialog on a regular basis with senior management.
- Ask questions of and critically review information provided by senior management, not just remain passive or a rubber stamp for senior management action.
- Define and communicate appropriate, and presumably objective measureable, performance and compensation standards for senior management consistent with the strategic objectives of the company.
- Ensure that senior management's knowledge and subject matter expertise remain suited to the strategic objectives of the business.
- Provide for succession and business continuity plans for senior management and other key employees. Banks in particular face increasing scrutiny on the depth and robustness of their plans related to these risks and are likely to continue to evaluate these issues as franchise risks going forward.

Makeup and Mechanics of the Board

The board should be purpose-built for the enterprise it proposes to serve and must be suitable to carry out its responsibilities. To do this, it must first have a composition that facilitates effective oversight. This means, and increasingly regulation requires (at least for public financial institutions), that the board have a sufficient number of independent directors.

The board should be comprised of individuals with a balance of skills, diversity, and expertise who collectively possess the necessary qualifications commensurate with the size, complexity, and risk profile of the bank.

In assessing the suitability of the board, we should consider:

- Membership should reflect a range of knowledge and experience in relevant areas and have varied backgrounds to promote a diversity of viewpoints. Relevant areas of competence include financial and capital markets, financial analysis, financial stability, customer service, technology, strategic planning, risk management, compensation, regulation, corporate governance, and management skills. The board should have a reasonable understanding of the economic and financial market forces at work in the markets where they operate and of the relevant legal and regulatory environment. Cross-border and international experience, where relevant, should also be considered. Where board expertise is insufficient in any of the above areas, the board should be able to employ independent subject matter experts as needed.

- Boards should have a clearly defined and substantive process for identifying, assessing, and selecting board candidates. The board (not senior management) should use a committee of independent directors to identify and nominate candidates and provide for appropriate succession planning of both board members and senior management. The evaluation and selection process should include reviewing whether board candidates have the knowledge, skills, experience, and independence of mind given their responsibilities on the board. And, in the light of the institution's business and risk profile, a board member should have a reputation for integrity and be free from litigation or reputational exposure with sufficient time to fully carry out her responsibilities (effectively limiting the number of outside boards one individual can serve).

- Board candidates should not have any conflicts of interest that may compromise their objectivity and/or subject them to undue influence from third parties, current or past senior management, or significant shareholders, a key concern in the era of the captive board and activist shareholders. Board members should also not be concentrated among a specific group or interest, foreclosing the possibility of cliques developing among members, which could potentially give rise to a conflict or act to the detriment of the company.

The Basel Committee on Banking Supervision, *Corporate Governance Principles for Banks*, recommends that in order to help board members acquire, maintain, and enhance their knowledge and skills, and fulfil their responsibilities, the board should ensure that members participate in orientation programs and have access to ongoing training on relevant issues. The board should dedicate sufficient time, budget, and other resources for this purpose, and draw on external expertise as needed. More extensive efforts should be made to train and keep updated those members with more limited financial, regulatory, or risk-related experience.

Effective and efficient administration dictates that the board structure itself, in terms of leadership, size, and the use of committees, so that it can effectively carry out its oversight role and related responsibilities. This includes ensuring that the board has the time and means to cover all necessary subjects in sufficient depth and have a cohesive and complete discussion of agenda-driven and ad-hoc issues. To serve this objective, the board should maintain, document, and periodically update its operating and organizational rules and memorialize its essential activities. To support its own performance, the board should carry out regular and routine assessments, either on a stand-alone basis or with the assistance of external subject matter experts. The board should, consistent with the reporting period of the institution (typically on an annual basis), periodically review its organizational structure, size, and composition and continuously evaluate the suitability of each board member either through peer review or with the help of independent subject matter experts. The results of this evaluation should drive efforts to improve the efficiency and effectiveness of the board in discussing, documenting, and deciding the top-of-house decisions that drive the company. Both regulators and shareholders may access these records, so it is critical that they be accurate and complete. The facilitator and manager of these activities, who plays a pivotal role, is the chair of the board. The chair provides leadership to the board and is responsible for its administrative and strategic efficiency and effectiveness. Consistent with any system of representative governance there should be distribution of administrative and hierarchical authority. Accordingly, the board chair should not be a member of senior management and should not serve as chair of any board committee. This separation of powers has been a focus of shareholder activists and regulators, so it is reasonable to expect evolution in this area.

To facilitate administrative efficiency and permit board members to focus on specific issues or areas of the business, the full board may authorize and establish certain specialized committees. The number and purpose of board committees depends upon several factors, including the size of the company, the nature of the business, and the risks that accompany it. Each committee of the board, indeed each committee in the company, should have a documentary charter defining its mandate, scope, and operating procedures. Consistent with the practices of the full board, each committee should document its plan or agenda and the product of its deliberations in the form of minutes and related expert reporting.

The core structure of board-level committees is driven by a combination of regulation, business structure, and strategy. The audit committee is perhaps the most common structure for financial institutions, being a requirement for systemically important banks and for those companies that are publicly traded by listing their securities on stock exchanges. For many financial institutions the function of overseeing the independent and internal auditors has been combined with oversight of regulatory examinations and interaction in a structure commonly identified as an audit and examinations committee. Key attributes of this committee include a makeup of independent, non-management directors with subject matter expertise so that the committee can approve the internal auditors plan and evaluate their findings, oversee accounting policies and internal controls, and also recommend the appointment and compensation of external auditors and provide oversight for the compliance function and interaction with regulators. For companies doing business in the United States, both the Foreign Corrupt Practices Act of 1977 and the Public Company Accounting Reform and Investor Protection Act (commonly known as Sarbanes-Oxley) hold senior and operating managers as well as the board of directors to stricter standards, including personal civil and criminal liability, related to their oversight of the activities, reporting, and internal controls of the organization.

Financial institutions such as banks, broker-dealers, swap dealers, and other regulated entities maintain and, where systemically important, are mandated by regulation to have a board-level risk committee with many of the same attributes as the audit committee. The risk committee is responsible for oversight of the risk appetite and related strategies together with the related policies and processes.

The Basel Committee on Banking Supervision, *Corporate Governance Principles for Banks*, noted in July 2015 that the risk committee of the board is responsible for advising the board on the bank's overall current and future risk appetite, overseeing senior management's implementation of the risk appetite statement, reporting on the state of risk culture in the bank, and interacting with and overseeing the chief risk officer. The risk committee's work includes oversight of the strategies for capital and liquidity management, as well as for all relevant risks of the bank, such as credit, market, operational, compliance, and reputational risks, to ensure they are consistent with the stated risk appetite. The committee should receive regular reporting and communication from the chief risk officer and other relevant functions about the bank's current risk profile, current state of the risk culture, utilization against the established risk appetite, and limit structure. The risk committee should meet periodically with the audit and other risk-relevant committees to ensure effective exchange of information and effective coverage of all risks, including emerging risks and any needed adjustments to the risk governance framework of the bank in the light of its business plans and the external environment.

Another key structure found on the board on many financial institutions and one that is similarly required of systemically important banks is the compensation committee. Regulatory reforms put in place in reaction to the 2008–2009 financial crisis mandate increased oversight of the compensation process, not only for banks, but for other types of institutions, such as swap dealers, as well. This committee is typically charged with overseeing the compensation system's design and operation, including the creation and functioning of incentive compensation awards, which in certain countries, including the United States, may be subject to statutory clawbacks.

Financial institutions may also maintain board-level committees to address issues and risks oriented to their specific business model. Institutions may increasingly maintain board-level committees to focus oversight on human resources/intellectual capital, information technology, and cybersecurity together with material conflicts of interest, business continuity, and disaster recovery.

The Role of Senior Management

Senior management consists of a core group of individuals who are responsible and accountable to the board for effectively overseeing the day-to-day management of the bank.

The organization and procedures and decision making of senior management should be clear and transparent and designed to promote effective management of the bank. This includes clarity on the role and authority of the various positions within senior management, including the CEO.

Members of senior management should have the necessary experience, competencies, and integrity to manage the businesses and people under their supervision. They should receive access to regular training to maintain and enhance their competencies and stay up to date on developments relevant to their areas of responsibility.

Members of senior management should be selected through an organizationally appropriate promotion and/or recruitment process that takes into account the full range of technical and interpersonal skills required for the particular position. For those senior management positions for which the board of directors is required to review or select candidates through an interview process, senior management should provide sufficient information to the board.

Senior management contributes substantially to a bank's sound corporate governance through personal conduct (e.g., by helping to set the "tone at the top" along with the board). Members of senior management should provide adequate oversight of those they manage, and ensure that the bank's activities are consistent with the business strategy, risk appetite, and the policies approved by the board.

Senior management is responsible for delegating duties to staff and should establish a management structure that promotes accountability and transparency throughout the bank.

Senior management should implement, consistent with the direction given by the board, risk management systems, processes, and controls for managing the risks—both financial and nonfinancial—to which the bank is exposed and for complying with laws, regulations, and internal policies. This includes comprehensive and independent risk management, compliance, and audit functions, as well as an effective overall system of internal controls.

The Role of Risk Management

The independent risk management function is a key component of the bank's second line of defense. This function is responsible for overseeing risk-taking activities across the enterprise. Key activities of the risk management function should include:

- Identifying material individual, aggregate, idiosyncratic, and emerging risks.
- Analyzing and assessing risks and measuring the company's exposure to them.
- Providing expertise and support to the board in its implementation, review, and approval of the enterprise-wide risk governance framework, which includes the company's risk culture, risk appetite, and limit structure.
- Monitoring and surveilling the risk-taking activities and risk exposures to determine if they are in line with the board-approved risk appetite, risk limits, and related capital or liquidity structure of the organization.
- Building out an early warning or trigger system for breaches of the risk appetite or limits structure both companywide as well as across an affiliated group of companies.
- Advising on and, when necessary, providing an effective second line of defense challenge to material risk decisions.
- Managing timely and complete reporting to senior management and the appropriate committee of the board, including but not limited to recommending appropriate actions to mitigate risk.

While it is standard practice for risk managers to work closely with or be embedded in individual business units, they should not be involved in or part of revenue-generating activities for the company. This separation acts to preserve the independence of the risk function. Such independence is an essential component of an effective risk management function, as is having access to all business lines and affiliated entities that can potentially generate material risk to the company.

As with each of the other control functions in the second and third line of defense, to competently execute their responsibilities, the risk management function should have enough qualified experienced staff to effectively challenge the business on the risks arising from revenue-generating or hedging activities.

The scope of the chief risk officer's (CRO) role has grown in tandem with that of financial institutions involved in multiple products or services, across markets, with growing or leveraged balance sheets, complex business structures, and increasing cross-border activity. The CRO, together with management and ultimately the board, should be actively engaged in establishing the risk appetite, policy, measures, and limits for the business and monitoring risk-taking against those limits. To adequately do this the CRO should be a participant in strategic planning, capital and liquidity planning, new products and services, compensation design, transaction settlement, and payment operation.

The CRO should have the organizational stature, authority, and necessary skills to oversee the bank's risk management activities. The CRO should be independent and have duties distinct from other executive functions. This requires the CRO to have access to any information necessary to perform his or her duties. The CRO, however, should not have management or financial responsibility related to any operational business lines or revenue-generating functions. Likewise, there should be no "dual hatting" (i.e., the chief operating officer, CFO, chief auditor, or other senior manager should, in principle, not also serve as the CRO). While formal reporting lines may vary across banks, the CRO should report and have direct access to the board or its risk committee without impediment. The CRO should have the ability to engage with the board and with senior management on key risk issues. Interaction between the CRO and the board and/or risk committee should occur regularly, and the CRO should have the ability to meet with the board or risk committee without executive directors (senior management) being present.

Changing the chief risk officer or head of any second-line control function should be subject to board oversight and may additionally be the subject of reporting to regulators. Further, it may be viewed as a disclosure event if the company is publicly traded.

A key lesson learned from the 2008–2009 financial crisis is that risk-taking by the enterprise should not, and must not, be allowed to get ahead of the policy framework and supporting infrastructure of the institution. This is critically true for banks and depository institutions because of the moral hazard of government-funded (read: taxpayer) bailout or stabilization. Prudence and safety and soundness dictate that the risk governance framework should include policies supported by appropriate control process and procedure designed to ensure that the institution's risk identification, aggregation, mitigation, and monitoring capabilities are commensurate with the size, complexity, and risk-absorbing capacity of the enterprise.

Risk identification should encompass all material risks to the bank, on- and off-balance-sheet and on group-wide, portfolio-wise, and business-line levels. In order to perform effective risk assessments, the board and senior management, including the CRO, should regularly and on an ad-hoc basis evaluate the risks faced by the bank and its overall risk profile. The risk assessment process should include ongoing analysis of existing risks as well as the identification of new or emerging risks. Risks should be captured from all organizational units that originate risk. Concentrations associated with material risks shall likewise be factored into the risk assessment.

The identification and measurement of risks should, to be complete, include both quantitative and qualitative elements. Risk measurements should also include qualitative, enterprise-wide views of risk relative to the institution's broader external operating environment; it is important not to underestimate the scope and breadth of the marketplace in which a particular company may operate and to appreciate the intermarket linkages that can lead to spillover or cascading of risks. Additionally, institutions should also have a methodology, including use of a workshop and scenario analysis, to identify and assign a value to important yet hard-to-measure risks, such as reputation risk and operational risk.

The system of internal controls should see to it that each identified risk has a policy, process, or other measure and a control to ensure that such policy, process, or other measure is being applied and works as intended. Accordingly, internal controls help ensure the integrity of the business process compliance with regulation and policy and overall process effectiveness. Internal controls should be designed to provide reasonable assurance that financial and management information is reliable, timely, and complete and that the institution is in compliance with relevant applicable laws, regulations, and policies. This point is particularly important in light of numerous attempts by governments and their regulatory agencies to apply their laws on an extraterritorial basis. Dodd-Frank and the European Union Market Abuse Regulation provide a good example of this type of action. In order to avoid unauthorized activity by employees or agents, or even fraud, internal controls should place reasonable checks and limits on managerial and employee actions. In smaller financial institutions, for example, key management decisions should be made by more than one individual. Periodic review and testing of an institution's compliance with company policies and procedures, together with related legal and regulatory policies, should be a core component of the system of internal controls. Additionally, credible and robust escalation procedures are likewise a key element of the internal control system.

The sophistication of a bank's or other financial institution's risk management infrastructure, including, most importantly, sufficiently robust data and data integrity, data architecture, and information technology infrastructure, should be carefully calibrated to keep pace with the introduction of new products or services, balance sheet and revenue growth, increasing complexity of the business model, risk rollup across legal entities, operating structure, and geographic or market expansion and mergers and acquisitions or joint ventures. Banks must have accurate internal and external data to identify and assess risk, make strategic business decisions, and determine capital and liquidity adequacy. The board and senior management should give special attention to the quality, completeness, and accuracy of the data used to make risk decisions.

The board and senior management own the risk for the enterprise. Their assessment of the risks and the methods for measurement of risks, both quantitative and qualitative, need to be reasonable and defensible based on observables and conventions in the broader environment. Accordingly, the BIS (Bank for International Settlements) notes that among others:

- Risk measurement and modeling techniques should be used in addition to, but should not replace, qualitative risk analysis and monitoring. The risk management function should keep the board and senior management apprised of the assumptions used in and potential shortcomings of the bank's risk models and analyses. This helps ensure a more complete and accurate reflection of exposures and may allow quicker action to address and mitigate risks.
- As part of its quantitative and qualitative analysis, the bank should utilize stress tests and scenario analyses to better understand potential risk exposures under a variety of adverse circumstances.[4]

Internal stress tests should cover a range of scenarios based on reasonable assumptions regarding dependencies and correlations. Senior management and, as applicable, the board should review and approve the scenarios that are used in the bank's risk analyses.

Stress test program results should be periodically reviewed with the board or its risk committee. Test results should be incorporated into the reviews of the risk appetite, the capital adequacy assessment process, the capital and liquidity planning processes, and budgets. They should also be linked to recovery and resolution planning. The risk management function should suggest if and what action is required based on results.

The results of stress tests and scenario analyses should also be communicated to, and given appropriate consideration by, relevant business lines and individuals within the bank.[5]

Banks should regularly compare actual performance against risk estimates (i.e., backtesting) to assist in judging the accuracy and effectiveness of the risk management process and making necessary adjustments.

In addition to identifying and measuring risk exposures, the risk management function should evaluate possible ways to mitigate these exposures.

In some cases, the risk management function may direct that risk be reduced or hedged to limit exposure. In other cases, such as when there is a decision to accept or take risk that is beyond risk limits (i.e., on a temporary basis) or take risk that cannot be hedged or mitigated, the risk management function should report and monitor the positions to ensure that they remain within the bank's framework of limits and controls or within exception approval. Either approach may be appropriate depending on the issue at hand, provided that the independence of the risk management function is not compromised.

Banks should have risk management and approval processes for new or expanded products or services, lines of business, and markets, as well as for large and complex transactions that require significant use of resources or have hard-to-quantify risks. Banks should also have review and approval processes for outsourcing bank functions to third parties. The risk management function should provide input on risks as part of such processes and on the outsourcer's ability to manage risks and comply with legal and regulatory obligations.

There needs to be a full and frank assessment of risks under a variety of scenarios, as well as an assessment of potential shortcomings in the ability of the bank's risk management and internal controls to effectively manage associated risks. As well, an assessment of the extent to which the bank's risk management, legal, and regulatory compliance, information technology, business line, and internal control functions have adequate tools and the expertise necessary to measure and manage related risks is important.

If adequate risk management processes are not in place, a new product, service, business line, or third-party relationship or major transaction should be delayed until the bank is able to appropriately address the activity. Effective risk management oversight entails continuously evaluating projected versus actual and updating both assumptions and reporting as needed, preferably within the structure of policy and process.

Additionally, the boards of affiliated and subsidiary companies and related senior management remain responsible for developing effective risk management processes and two-way channels of communication and reporting for each member of a corporate group. The methods and procedures applied by subsidiaries should be consistent and support the effectiveness of risk management at an enterprise-wide level. While parent companies should conduct strategic, group-wide risk management and specify corporate risk policies, subsidiary management and boards may differ depending upon the type of regulated entity involved (i.e., broker-dealer, swap dealer, futures commission merchant, etc.) and their assessment of local and business risks.

COMMUNICATION IN THE ORGANIZATION

Effective governance of the enterprise requires dynamic communication of and about risk both hierarchically and across the organization. Dynamic communication is a foundation of a strong risk culture. A strong risk culture should promote systemic and situational risk awareness and lead, not restrict, open communication and an effective second line of defense challenge about risk-taking both up and down as well as across the institution. The organizational bias should be to push information rather than wait for pull or inquiry. A lesson learned from the financial crisis is that isolation or siloing within the institution can interfere with efficient and effective communication of necessary information with potentially bad decisions the obvious result. Tone from the top matters when it comes to opening and maintaining channels of communication, so that accurate, relevant, concise, and contextual information is presented to decision makers in senior management and the board when needed.

Material risk-related ad-hoc information that requires immediate decisions or reactions should be promptly presented to senior management and the board, the responsible officers, and, where applicable, the heads of control functions, so that suitable measures and activities can be initiated at an early stage. Suitable policies and procedures should be established for this purpose.

Risk reporting to the board requires careful design in order to ensure that bankwide, individual portfolio, and other risks are conveyed in a concise and meaningful manner. Reporting should accurately communicate risk exposures and results of stress tests or scenario analyses and should provoke a robust discussion of, for example, the bank's current and prospective exposures (particularly under stressed scenarios), risk/return relationships, and risk appetite and limits. Reporting should also include information about the external environment to identify market conditions and trends that may have an impact on the bank's current or future risk profile.

Risk reporting systems should be dynamic, comprehensive, and accurate, and should draw on a range of underlying assumptions. Risk monitoring and reporting should not only occur at the disaggregated level (including risk residing in subsidiaries that could be considered significant), but should also be aggregated to allow for a bankwide or integrated perspective of risk exposures. Risk reporting systems should be clear about any deficiencies or limitations in risk estimates, as well as any significant embedded assumptions (e.g., regarding risk dependencies or correlations).

COMPLIANCE

Different types of financial institutions and regulated entities—banks, broker-dealers, swap dealers, futures commission merchants, and others—require some measure of interaction between the governance structure—the board of directors and senior management—and a formal compliance function.[6]

An independent, credible compliance function is a key component of the institution's second line of defense. The compliance and regulatory function is responsible, among other things, for promoting and monitoring that the entity operates with integrity and in compliance with applicable laws, regulations, and policies. Implicit in this idea is that there are systems and processes for management, supervision, communication, and escalation as well as reporting. As with other elements of the governance structure, achieving a culture of compliance starts at the top of the organization with a board and senior management that lead by example. Communication is critical in engaging all levels of the company in adopting the compliance culture: People everywhere in the company need to know what's right and what is not and what to do about it if there's a problem. Needless to say, communication and training, both formal and informal, go hand in hand in achieving this goal.

The Basel Committee on Banking Supervision issued compliance guidelines, for banks in particular, providing in part that a bank should hold itself to high standards when carrying out its business and should at all times strive to observe the spirit as well as the letter of the law. Failure to consider the impact of its actions on its shareholders, customers, employees, and the markets may result in significant adverse publicity and reputational damage, even if no law has been broken.

The bank's senior management is responsible for establishing a written compliance approach and policies that contain the basic principles to be followed by the board, management, and staff, and explains the main processes by which compliance risks are to be identified and managed through all levels of the organization. Clarity and transparency may be promoted by making a distinction between general standards for all staff members and rules that only apply to specific groups of staff.

While the board and management are accountable for the bank's compliance, the compliance function has an important role in supporting corporate values, policies, and processes that help ensure that the bank acts responsibly and observes all obligations applicable to it.

The compliance function should advise the board and senior management on compliance laws, rules, and standards, including keeping them informed of developments in the area. It should also help educate staff about compliance issues, act as a contact point within the bank for compliance queries from staff members, and provide guidance to staff on the appropriate implementation of compliance laws, rules, and standards in the form of policies and procedures and other documents such as compliance manuals, internal codes of conduct, and practice guidelines.

The compliance function is independent from management and provides separate reporting to the board on the bank's efforts in the above areas and on how the bank is managing its compliance risk. Broker-dealer and swap-dealer rules adopt a similar approach with certain procedural differences.

To be effective, the compliance function must have sufficient authority, stature, independence, resources, and access to the board. Management should respect the independent duties of the compliance function and not interfere with them.[7]

Additionally, given the constantly changing nature of the business environment in which financial institutions operate and the convergence of issues across the regulatory, legal, and risk spectrum, compliance should always be proactive and prepared to focus on new, emerging, or idiosyncratic issues that could create regulatory or reputational risk for the institution. This includes bribery and corruption, money laundering and terrorist financing, sanctioned regimes, and fair treatment of the retail customers or consumers as well as business practices raising ethical issues, actions that, simply put, don't pass the sight and smell test.

INTERNAL AUDIT

Of all types of financial institutions, banks have the most robust relationship with the internal audit function. The Basel Committee on Banking Supervision notes that the internal audit function provides independent assurance to the board and supports board and senior management in promoting an effective governance process and the long-term soundness of the bank.

Banks, public companies, other financial institutions, and regulated entities are in agreement that the internal audit function should have a clear mandate, acknowledged by the board and establishing accountability to the board, be independent of the audited activities, and have sufficient standing, skills, resources, and authority within the enterprise. The board and senior management should recognize and acknowledge that an independent and qualified internal audit function is vital to an effective governance process.

An effective internal audit function provides an independent assurance to the board of directors and senior management on the quality and effectiveness of a bank's internal control, risk management, and governance systems and processes, thereby helping the board and senior management protect their organization and its reputation.[8]

The internal audit function should be accountable to the board on all matters related to the performance of its mandate as described in the internal audit charter. It must be independent of the audited activities and have sufficient standing, authority, and resources within the bank to enable the auditors to carry out their assignments effectively and objectively.

The board and senior management can enhance the effectiveness of the internal audit function by:

- Requiring the function to independently assess the effectiveness and efficiency of the internal control, risk management, and governance systems and processes.
- Requiring internal auditors to adhere to national and international professional standards, such as those established by the Institute of Internal Auditors and the Securities & Financial Markets Association.
- Ensuring that audit staff have skills and resources commensurate with the business activities and risks of the bank.
- Requiring timely and effective correction of audit issues by senior management.
- Requiring a periodic assessment of the bank's overall risk governance framework, including, but not limited to, an assessment of the effectiveness of the risk management and compliance functions; the quality of risk reporting to the board and senior management; and the effectiveness of the bank's system of internal controls.

The board and senior management should respect and promote the independence of the internal audit function by, for example, ensuring that internal audit reports are provided to the board without first being filtered by management and that the internal auditors have direct access to the board or the board's audit committee.

COMPENSATION: THE HOT BUTTON ISSUE

Compensation systems form a key component of the governance and incentive structure through which the board and senior management promote good performance, convey acceptable risk-taking behavior, and reinforce the bank's operating and risk culture. The board is responsible for the overall oversight of the compensation system for the entire bank. In addition, the board should regularly monitor and review outcomes to ensure that the bankwide compensation system is operating as intended. The board should review the compensation policy at least annually.[9]

Consistent with the Financial Stability Board's (FSB) *Principles for Sound Compensation Practices* and the listing standards of many securities exchanges, the board should approve the compensation of senior executives, including the CEO, CRO, and the head of internal audit, and should oversee management's development and operation of compensation policies, systems, and related control processes that promote conflict-free, long-term employee performance consistent with the interests of the company and its risk appetite.

Significant financial institutions should have a board remuneration committee as an integral part of their governance structure and organization to oversee the compensation system's design and operation on behalf of the board of directors. The remuneration committee should be constituted in a way that enables it to exercise competent and independent judgment on compensation policies and practices and the incentives created for managing risk, capital, and liquidity. For employees in risk, compliance, and other control functions, compensation should be determined independently of any business line overseen, and performance measures should be based principally on the achievement of their own objectives so as not to compromise their independence.[10]

A persistent issue beginning with the start of the 1980s bull market and continuing through the 2008–2009 financial crisis is matching the compensation paid with the risk put on the books of the company. Practices by which compensation is paid for potential future revenues whose timing and likelihood remain uncertain should be carefully evaluated by means of both qualitative and quantitative key indicators. Banks and depository institutions should ensure that contingent or variable compensation is adjusted to take into account the full range of current and potential risks an employee takes as well as realized risks, including breaches of internal procedures or legal requirements. Common sense though it may be, total compensation should reflect risk-taking and risk outcomes for the employee as well as the institution.

Compensation payout schedules should be sensitive to risk outcomes over a multiyear horizon. This is often achieved through arrangements that defer a sufficiently large part of the compensation for a sufficiently long period of time until risk outcomes become better known. This includes "malus/forfeiture" provisions (where compensation can be reduced or reversed based on realized risks or conduct events before compensation vests) and/or clawback provisions under which compensation can be reduced or reversed after compensation vests if new facts emerge that the compensation paid was based on erroneous assumptions (such as misreporting) or if it is discovered that the employee has failed to comply with internal policies or legal requirements. "Golden Halo's" or "golden parachutes," under which new or terminated executives or staff receive large payouts irrespective of performance, are generally not consistent with sound compensation practice.

DISCLOSURE AND REPORTING

For any financial institution, particularly banks and those that are publicly traded, transparency and disclosure governance should be a top, if not the top, concern. A company should be adequately transparent to shareholders, depositors, counterparties, vendors, other relevant stakeholders, and market participants. Anyone with doubts about the need for adequate scope and breadth of transparency should look no further than Enron and Lehman Brothers. When it comes to banks, transparency is consistent with sound and effective corporate governance of any institution. It is difficult for shareholders, depositors, other relevant stakeholders, and market participants to effectively monitor and properly hold the board and senior management accountable when there is insufficient transparency. The objective of transparency in the area of corporate governance is therefore to provide these parties with the information necessary to enable them to assess the effectiveness of the board and senior management in governing the bank.[11]

Although disclosure may be less detailed for non-publicly traded institutions, especially those that are wholly owned, these institutions, some of which are banks, can nevertheless pose the same types of risk to the financial system as publicly traded banks through various activities, including their participation in payment systems and acceptance of retail deposits. All banks, even those for whom disclosure requirements may differ because they are nonlisted, should disclose relevant and useful information that supports the key areas of corporate governance. Such disclosure should be proportionate to the size, complexity, structure, economic significance, and risk profile of the bank. This is particularly relevant in the community bank space where many institutions are not publicly held or not public reporting companies.[12]

SUMMARY

In order to credibly and adequately govern a financial institution, the board should lead the oversight of the company's strategic objectives, including risk appetite, financial performance, capital adequacy, capital planning, liquidity, risk profile and risk culture, controls, compensation practices, and the selection and evaluation of management. The board should also manage oversight of risk management's control, compliance, and internal audit functions as well. By executing against these tasks, a credible case can be made that there exists a governance framework for the financial institution.

NOTES

1. Basel Committee on Banking Supervision, *Corporate Governance Principles for Banks*, July 2015, p. 7.
2. Ibid., p. 8.
3. Basel Committee on Banking Supervision, *Principles for Effective Risk Data Aggregation and Risk Reporting*, January 2013.
4. Basel Committee on Banking Supervision, *Corporate Governance Principles for Banks*, July 2015, p. 25.
5. Basel Committee on Banking Supervision, *Principles for Governance of Banks*, July 2015, p. 25.
6. Basel Committee on Banking Supervision, *Compliance and the Compliance Function in Banks*, 2005.
7. Basel Committee on Banking Supervision, *Principles for Governance of Banks*, June 2015, p. 28.
8. Basel Committee on Banking Supervision, *The Internal Audit Function in Banks*, 2012.
9. Basel Committee on Banking Supervision, *Principles for Governance of Banks*, June 2015, p. 30.
10. Financial Stability Board, *The FSB Principles for Sound Compensation Practices and Their Implementation Standards*—Report of August 2013, p. 14.
11. Financial Stability Board, *Enhancing the Risk Disclosures of Banks-Report of the Enhanced Disclosure Task Force*, October 2012.
12. Basel Committee on Banking Supervision, *Principles for Governance of Banks*, June 2015, p. 32.

CHAPTER 4

Overview: Capital Markets Compliance

Firms engaged in capital markets activities are required to comply with the laws, rules, and regulations applicable to their regulated business and to have a comprehensive compliance program to address the risks inherent in the business activities in which they engage. The end goal of the compliance program is to prevent violations of laws, rules, and regulations, to deter employees from engaging in inappropriate acts that may place the firm at risk of violating laws, rules, and regulations applicable to its business. To accomplish this, a firm must identify weaknesses in various businesses (e.g., recurring violations of laws, rules, or regulations, employees engaging in illegal activities and/or business practices conducted outside of industry standards of conduct or best practices) and remedy any control weaknesses that are identified. The firm then implements an ongoing system that monitors business activities in order to provide senior management and/or the board of directors or equivalent governing body with the confidence that the firm has a reasonable compliance program to enable it to comply with laws, rules, regulations, and standards of conduct in the business activities engaged in by the firm.

While business supervisors are considered the first line of defense in a firm's mission to implement an effective compliance program, firms also employ compliance departments (which, along with the risk management function, represent the second line of defense) to implement compliance programs and work with senior management to ensure the firm complies with its various legal and regulatory obligations and implements fundamentally sound business practices. For the most part, compliance departments support and work with the senior business leaders to provide advice, train employees, and monitor activities to assist the senior leaders with their vast responsibilities in supervising the day-to-day business activities regardless of whether the firm is small and engaged in certain niche activities, medium-sized and operating in a few, but not all, capital market activities, or one of the mammoth financial institutions engaged in a vast array of global business activities.

DIFFERENTIATION BETWEEN COMPLIANCE AND LEGAL DEPARTMENTS

Compliance departments are independent control functions. They, generally, do not report to business lines due to the conflicts that can arise. For example, if the compliance officer reports to a business head who determines the salary and annual bonus for the compliance officer, there is the possibility that a business head could pressure a compliance officer to make advisory decisions during the year that would benefit the business head, regardless of the regulatory implications, and the compliance officer would fear that adverse decisions might affect the compliance officer's income. Compliance departments should also avoid reporting to a senior business head to avoid the appearance that the compliance department is in the business line's supervision purview and the perception that the compliance department is an extension of business supervision. Such inherent risks will be discussed later in this overview of compliance responsibilities.

The head of compliance or chief compliance officer should only supervise other compliance officers. The compliance department should report through another control function such as legal or risk management. The compliance department should be led by a head of compliance or chief compliance officer who should supervise other compliance officers (and no business functions). To describe the purpose of the compliance department, the compliance department should draft a mission statement and/or procedure manual that clearly defines the structure of the compliance department, the role that compliance plays in the organization, the function and responsibilities of individual compliance officers, and what responsibilities are not within the purview of the compliance department.

A concept that is confusing to many employees within a capital markets firm or division is the role of a compliance department. Many employees of financial capital markets firms (aside from the legal and compliance departments) don't understand the difference between the legal and compliance departments and, hence, don't understand the function of the compliance department. One contributing factor is that as regulation steadily increased over time, culminating with the financial crisis of 2007–2008, financial institutions required highly skilled personnel with the ability to read, interpret, and communicate to employees complicated and voluminous laws, rules, and regulations as well as assisting businesses in the application of these regulatory schemes to a firm's business. As a result, compliance departments are increasingly staffed with lawyers and law school graduates. This seems to cause some confusion among some people within the financial services industry as to the difference in the roles and responsibilities between legal and compliance departments.

This also creates problems for compliance and legal department team members as there are times when a business-side employee looking for advice—and not being clear to which department it should direct the question—will pose an interpretive question to both legal and compliance personnel. In some instances, the employee does not inform the other department that both have been posed with the identical question. The confusion begins if the answers provided differ, creating confusion among the business-side employees as they may be unclear as to which advice is accurate, and it may cause them to question the advice provided by both departments. As the ability to engage in certain transactions with large, sophisticated institutions and counterparties may require quick and decisive legal and compliance department advice in order to execute a transaction, it is possible a transaction may be lost to inconsistent advice and that can reflect negatively on the perceived quality of the legal and compliance departments' advice. Customers may subsequently believe they cannot engage in more complicated transactions with the firm if it can't get a decisive decision on whether a transaction can be executed with the firm or it takes too long for the capital markets department to get comfortable with the legal and/or compliance issues involved in a transaction.

Another issue raised by this scenario is that more aggressive business personnel may use the inconsistent advice to their advantage by ignoring the advice least beneficial to them and comply with the advice that best fits their needs. These issues make it imperative that a firm clearly delineate the responsibilities of the compliance department and ensure that it is clear how it differs from the legal department.

The legal department in a capital markets firm is tasked with providing legal advice and interpretation on legal issues that affect a respective business. For example, a legal department will address state and federal law issues, draft contracts, and assist the business in drafting agreements with respect to customers (e.g., customer account agreements and corporate finance and mergers-and-acquisitions engagement letters).

ROLES AND RESPONSIBILITIES OF THE CHIEF COMPLIANCE OFFICER

The chief compliance officer (CCO) is the primary advisor to senior management and is responsible for implementing the firm's overall compliance program. The CCO must assess the risks the firm faces in the business activities that it engages and advise management on a reasonable program to address the related compliance risks. Some compliance risks a CCO must consider during implementation of his compliance program as well as some tools he will need to address such risks include:

- A robust anti–money laundering (AML) program with a knowledgeable AMLCO and support team that understands the business activities engaged in by the firm and can identify and address compliance risk issues that rise from such business as they relate to AML and sanctions rules and regulations.
- An automated, intelligent surveillance program to quickly identify compliance weaknesses within the business units.
- A compliance monitoring program to independently test the effectiveness of the policies, procedures, and written supervisory procedures as well as verify that management implements a program to address and promptly implement corrective measures to address issues or exceptions noted throughout the monitoring program.
- An effective registration and licensing department to understand the multitude of licensing requirements applicable to a firm and its employees and to ensure the firm and employees are adequately licensed as required by the various self-regulating organizations (SROs), exchanges, alternative trading systems (ATSs), and market centers.
- A robust training program for employees to ensure all personnel are well trained on the firm's policies and procedures as well as relevant laws, rules, and regulations applicable to the firm's business activities. In addition, the training program should assist management in implementing the regulatory element of training required by FINRA as well as the training programs required by the various self-regulatory bodies and exchanges.
- A program of business activity reviews to assess the effectiveness of policies and procedures and compliance programs of individual businesses and branch offices.
- A regulatory examination team to handle the regulatory examination process and the numerous document production and other requests that occur during regulatory examinations.
- A regulatory inquiry team to be the main contact for regulators in their periodic requests for information from the firm. This would also include coordinating with the firm's business teams in obtaining background information and explanations to regulatory inquiries, coordinating with the business and operations groups that maintain the books and records related to a regulatory inquiry, and drafting persuasive responses to regulatory inquiries to address the regulators' concerns.

- Implementing an effective control room to manage the vast amounts of MNPI (material non-public information) that the firm may receive, ensuring "Chinese Walls" and other information barriers are implemented firmwide to control the flow of MNPI and periodically testing the effectiveness of such information barriers.
- Implementing an effective ethics program to verify that all employees are complying with firm policies and procedures. This would include implementation of an employee personal trading program to monitor the personal securities investments of employees and ensure that employees in possession of firm MNPI do not effect personal securities transactions in violation of the insider trading laws. Additional aspects of the ethics program may include monitoring the various activities or investments employees engage in outside of their employment with the firm—for example, private placement investments, employment outside of the firm, memberships on boards of directors, and so forth—to ensure such activities don't result in employees taking advantage of opportunities that should be offered to the firm or employees don't engage in activities that may negatively affect the firm or the firm's customers, or result in negative news about the firm to customers or the general public.

The CCO must also engage in a practice of assessing the compliance program's ongoing effectiveness, identify any weaknesses present, develop a remediation plan for such weaknesses (along with the senior business leaders), and report such progress to senior management. Within FINRA-registered broker-dealers, this generally occurs as part of the annual testing of supervisory controls and the CCO report to senior management completed as part of the requirements pursuant to FINRA Rule 3120 on Supervisory Control Systems and FINRA Rule 3130, requiring an Annual Certification of Compliance and Supervisory Processes. This type of assessment should also be conducted at non-broker-dealer financial firms as the compliance assessment required is a necessary component to testing the effectiveness of a firm's compliance program.

ROLES AND RESPONSIBILITIES OF THE COMPLIANCE DEPARTMENT

The compliance department has multifaceted roles. Some compliance officers may be imbedded in a business and others may work in a centralized compliance function. We will explore the various roles and responsibilities of these functions within a capital markets structure.

Advisory Function

The primary role of this function is to advise employees on the laws, rules, and regulations applicable to the firm's business. For example, if the entity is a Securities and Exchange Commission (SEC)–regulated broker-dealer that is a member of a self-regulatory organization such as Financial Industry Regulatory Authority (FINRA) or the New York Stock Exchange (NYSE), then the compliance department should be knowledgeable in the relevant rules and regulations of those entities and provide advice to employees on such rules and regulations as they apply to the firm's business and transactional activity. If the firm legal entity is a swaps dealer regulated by the Commodities Futures Trading Commission (CFTC) and a member of the self-regulatory organization, the National Futures Association (NFA), then employees should be knowledgeable in the rules and regulations of those organizations and be able to provide advice on their rules and regulations and their applicability to the capital markets business.

An example of the type of advice that may be requested of a compliance officer is:

- A salesperson of the firm may be approached by a retail customer who has multiple accounts with the firm. The customer has a security in one of her accounts and would like to move those securities to another account. In addition, she would like to sell the securities from the first account to the second account at a price well above the current market price. The salesperson may have numerous questions, such as, can the firm engage in this transaction and sell the securities from one account to another when there is no beneficial change in ownership in the sale transaction? Even if it is permissible, can the firm execute such a transaction at a price that is different from the current prevailing market? The compliance officer can reference the FINRA, NYSE, and other related laws, rules, and regulations that will speak to the permissibility of such a transaction.

Another example may be:

- An institutional salesperson receiving a call from a hedge fund located in Latvia that knows the firm's high-yield trading desk owns a bond in a certain credit that the account has interest in and would like to buy such bonds. The institutional salesperson would normally go through the new account opening process of the firm and then sell the customer such bonds. However, since this account is located in Latvia, the salesperson knows the firm does not maintain a broker-dealer license in Latvia and is unaware of the country's regulations related to foreign entities selling securities into Latvia that do not have licenses to engage in such activities in that country. The compliance officer should determine whether the firm is permitted to sell securities into Latvia. If not, are there any such Latvian regulations prohibiting this or, if there is a regulation that requires the firm to have such a license to sell securities into Latvia, are there any exemptions that may allow the firm to sell securities to an institutional account in Latvia? In addition, are there any U.S. or global government sanctions against Latvia or the specific account within Latvia that may prevent the firm from opening an account and transacting securities with the hedge fund?

Monitoring

Periodic testing or "monitoring" of business activities is a good way for the firm to test the controls that it has in place. This might include a deep-dive review of a specific business within capital markets (e.g., equity trading, fixed-income trading, options trading, debt capital markets, mergers and acquisitions, corporate finance, government securities trading, municipal securities, public finance activities, etc.). The purpose is to support senior management in its responsibility to adequately supervise the business activities of the firm. These monitoring reviews are generally "independent" reviews conducted by a control group like compliance to assess whether businesses are engaging in activities in compliance with relative laws, rules, regulations, policies, and procedures and to test that supervisors are adequately supervising such activities. Any issues identified and subsequent corrective action implemented as a result of these monitoring reviews can be incorporated into the supervisor's daily supervision responsibilities.

An example may be:

- A compliance officer may take a period of time in the past. (For example, if it decides to review fixed-income trading, it might review the previous one month of trading activity in all fixed-income products, or maybe six months of activity; or if it is reviewing public finance activities, it might select as a test sample all transactions that occurred during 2016.) In this monitoring exercise, the focus may be to look at all of the FINRA, SEC, and Municipal Securities Rulemaking Board (MSRB) rules and regulations that apply to the business area and apply those rules to the transactions that it reviews. It should summarize the testing and reviews conducted in a memorandum addressed to the business head. Any issues or exceptions that are noted will be described in such report, and senior management will be asked to respond in writing as to how it intends to correct such issues and in what time frame those issues will be repaired.

Management will provide a written response with its corrective action. The details of the review, issues, exceptions, and remedial action will be documented in the memorandum to memorialize this monitoring review.

Surveillance

Surveillance of business transactions as well as e-communications is another method of testing the firm's supervisory controls. While some firms may conduct surveillance outside of the compliance department and in a unit that reports directly to business lines or supervisors, many firms have surveillance rest within the compliance department. A compliance officer may work with supervisors and the information technology department to create reports or systems that will track or monitor capital markets transactions on a real-time basis (as they are happening) to help identify whether any anomalies occur, if improper behavior is being engaged in by salespersons or traders, if less-than-optimal execution is being provided to customers, and whether salespeople and traders are engaging in any practices that would violate any laws, rules, and regulations or industry best practices or standards of conduct.

For example:

- It is very important for any equity trading desk to have policies, procedures, and written supervisory procedures to ensure that the firm provides optimal or "best" execution to its customers who transact with the firm in equity securities. The firm needs a system to ensure that it satisfies its obligations under the best execution regulations that FINRA, NYSE, or another self-regulatory body has established for its members. An active equity trading desk could have daily executions in the millions per day; it would be virtually impossible to expect the limited number of equity trading supervisors to be able to manually review each trade executed by the firm's trading desk and verify the pricing satisfies its best-execution obligations. Most equity trading firms have electronic order management systems (OMSs) whereby the salespeople enter orders into the system upon receipt from customer, and the OMS has a logic that routes the order either to the trading desk or into the market, to the market center or exchange that will execute the order at the best market price at the time the order is received by the execution facility. In order to test for the quality of the execution, firms utilize systematic surveillance solutions whereby they create their own system or utilize a system provided by a third-party vendor that can capture all of the transactions (as well as all transaction details) executed by the firm each day. These systems generally also have the ability to receive an electronic feed of market pricing throughout the day and isolate the inside market (i.e., highest bid and lowest offer for a quoted size) for each equity security at each second throughout the day. The systems will then compare each of the firm's executions to the inside market at the specific second that the firm executed an order to determine whether the firm provided its customer with an execution price at or within the inside market at the specific instance that the firm executed its customer order during the day. The logic in a best-execution system can then highlight or flag an item that is executed outside of the inside market at the time it is executed. These "exceptions" to best execution can either be printed on an exception report or be systematically flagged to a supervisor at the time the customer order is executed (i.e. on a real-time basis) as an exception whereby the supervisor would be instructed to take some action. That action may include amending the customer execution price or canceling the execution to the customer due to its less-than-optimal pricing; or the supervisor may believe the execution is at an optimal price for the customer, and the surveillance system may require a supervisor to explain why the price is an optimal price at the time (e.g., there may have been extreme volatility and/or volume in the market at the time of execution causing delays in the time of order receipt and execution; or there may be delays in the information the surveillance system is receiving, and the price when it was executed was actually within the inside market at the time but the system is having trouble absorbing so much market information in a timely manner).

Another example of a surveillance report or system may be for e-communications:

■ A firm may implement a surveillance system for all e-mails, instant messages, Bloomberg, Reuters, or other common chat or electronic communications. The e-surveillance system can collect all electronic communications and feed them into a lexicon system that recognizes certain words, phrases, and/or characteristics and flag or quarantine all such communications and require a reviewer (generally, a compliance officer or a supervisor) to review and approve such communications before they can be released to customers (if the system requires preapproval of certain communications) or to be reviewed after the communication has been sent. In some firms, these electronic communications must first be reviewed by the compliance officer, and they will involve a supervisor if they believe further action is necessary. In other firms, this would initially reside with a supervisory function and may involve compliance if a supervisor has concerns with an employee's electronic communications. A reviewer will go into such a system and review the flagged or quarantined communications and will be required to document any action she took regarding such communication. The actions may include approving such communication because the e-mail did not contain concerning language in the context it was sent, or it was approved for distribution because the concerning word or phrase was included in an e-mail disclaimer or attachment and was not communicated to a customer in an inappropriate manner, or the reviewer either spoke with the employee sender or took further action such as referring the communication to a senior supervisor, reprimanding the employee, or referring the employee to human resources for additional action or training.

Training

Training is one of the core compliance functions. The compliance department administers training to firm personnel on policies, procedures, firm codes of conduct, existing regulations, and new and emerging regulations, as well as administering the regulatory element continuing education training requirement implemented by various self-regulatory organizations such as FINRA (FINRA Rule 1120) and NYSE (NYSE Rule 345A). The compliance department will also work with supervisory personnel on developing an annual training needs analysis, which will detail the various businesses that the firm conducts and the relevant and emerging rules and regulations that are applicable to those businesses. The plan will then identify the personnel within specific businesses and prepare relevant training on laws, rules, regulations, policies, and procedures applicable to that business with the business supervisor and/or assign via online continuing education training modules.
    For example:

- The underwriting business unit might be assigned training that covers securities registration requirements under the Securities Act of 1933 or the private placement exemptions from registration that are available to issuers. Fixed-income trading personnel might receive training on the TRACE fixed-income trade reporting obligations of FINRA member firms or on the best-execution requirement applicable for fixed-income securities.

Business Activity Reviews

Compliance officers also engage in business activity reviews based on the businesses that a specific compliance officer covers. The purpose of these reviews is to identify any potential regulatory violations, inappropriate conduct being engaged in by sales and trading personnel, or any operational deficiencies that may be occurring. These reviews may be conducted in concert with other control groups.

For example:

- A compliance officer may review the personal securities trading activities of sales and trading personnel to ensure there are no conflicts such as employees tasked with preparing equity research reports engaging in transactions that contrast with the recommendations they have made in public research reports. If a research analyst prepares a report for customers that provides a sell recommendation in Apple stock at current prices due to emerging problems with the company yet the same research analyst is buying the stock in his or her personal account, that would be conflict that a compliance officer would want to escalate to senior management.

The compliance department may also review certain supervisory actions to make sure the actions of supervisors are consistent with the firm's goal of reasonable supervision.

For example:

- A compliance officer may review the actions of supervisors in best-execution exceptions to verify that they are conducting their supervision obligations and those actions appear reasonable. Or they may review the supervisory actions taken in the e-communication surveillance system to make sure the supervisors have reviewed flagged communications and whether they believed the supervisor's actions were reasonable. This compliance officer review acts as an independent check on supervisors. If the compliance found an action that he or she did not agree with, then the compliance officer would refer the matter to the supervisor's supervisor to ensure he or she also reviews and takes appropriate action on the matter. Such actions may include confirming the supervisor's action as reasonable or taking some form of disciplinary action on the original sender and possibly the supervisor for not adequately supervising the e-communication review.

Another type of business review conducted by the compliance department are branch office reviews. Each FINRA-regulated broker-dealer has an obligation to review each branch office generally, annually, or every three years depending upon the activities engaged in by the branch and whether a branch is a supervisory location (i.e., an office of supervisory jurisdiction). The compliance department, on behalf of the firm, will do a complete review of the activities and personnel at each branch office to make sure all activities are conducted within firm policies and procedures as well as all relevant laws, rules, regulations, and standards of conduct. This would include a top-to-bottom review of business activities, which may include: Testing a sample of all trading activities occurring at the branch as well as sampling activity in customer accounts covered by the branch office and reviewing against regulatory requirements, sampling customer account activity during a defined period of time and reviewing trading conducted in such accounts for any inappropriate activity engaged in by the customer or the firm salesperson that covers those accounts, reviewing the securities licensing status of all personnel located in the office to ensure they maintain appropriate licenses for the activities they engage in, reviewing the personal trading of all office personnel during a certain test period to make sure there is not any unusual activity, and reviewing any outside business activities of such personnel to make sure these do not conflict with their position at the firm or cause a conflict with the business engaged in by the firm.

Anti–Money Laundering

Anti–money laundering (AML) is another function handled by the compliance department as compliance administers the firm's AML program. The main responsibility in a regulated entity resides with the anti–money laundering compliance officer (AMLCO), which is a designated title within most regulated entities. The AMLCO, and other compliance officers who report to the AMLCO or are responsible for AML compliance, will draft the AML policies and procedures for the firm. These outline how the firm addresses the opening and/or approval of new accounts, any special policies and/or procedures that may be applicable to new and existing accounts in countries or regions that are considered high-risk for money-laundering activities, any special considerations if the account owner is a politically exposed person (e.g., a current or former government official, head of state, or related person), and how the firm will administer the global and U.S. government sanctions that may be applicable to certain entities, individuals, and countries. In addition, the AMLCO will implement a surveillance program to monitor for suspicious customer transactions involving the movement of funds and assets (e.g., securities).

For example:

- The movement of funds by customers—whether between their accounts at the firm or to an account at another bank or in the form of a customer wiring funds to pay certain bills—is an operational function and the transaction is performed and approved in an operations department.

However, if a customer is wiring funds to a third party not affiliated with the customer or a customer account or to a country that is high-risk for AML, the firm's procedures may require that additional due diligence be done by the wire team and/or the salesperson covering the account to find the relationship between the sender and receiver and the purpose of the payment. In addition, the AML policies may require the AMLCO to approve any wire to an unaffiliated third party prior to it being sent.

Another example:

- The AMLCO should implement a system to review the firm's receipt of low-priced securities. Certain customers may request that the firm take a free delivery of low-priced securities into their account—meaning that the customer, or a related party, will delivery securities to the firm for the account of the customer and the customer will not have to pay for them because the delivering party is not requesting payment for delivery. A free delivery of low-priced or penny-stock securities and a quick sale has been one way that certain stock promoters and company insiders have sold stock after manipulating the price of a stock. In some cases, the promoter (who may also be an insider) has worked to artificially raise or "pump up" the price of the stock to the highest price possible, and when they believe it is at its highest price, they sell their shares into the market to receive the highest possible value; and then the stock retreats in price or plummets in price after the manipulation is over and the price falls to its actual value or market price. While it's certainly possible that the customer received these shares in a legitimate transaction such as a gift or maybe even as payment for participation in a transaction with the issuer as a lender or equity contributor, the firm needs to make sure that it is not being used by a customer in an illegitimate transaction to launder funds from another illegitimate transaction to make those funds "clean" by distancing the money from the illegal transaction and generating "clean" cash in a legitimate transaction—the sale to securities.

With an increasing amount of sanctions against firms and AMLCOs for inadequacies in their AML program, AMLCOs must ensure their AML programs address the following issues:

- Ensuring the firm's procedures are tailored to address the risks of the firm's businesses and customers and not procedures that are general in nature or addressed to types of businesses or customers not handled by the firm.

- Implementing a customer identification program that is thorough, detailed, and sufficient to accurately verify underlying customers' identity.
- Implementing a program to identify suspicious activity and/or transactions and filing suspicious activity reports with the Treasury Department's Financial Crimes Enforcement Network (FinCEN) when necessary. Many firms today implement programs whereby there is an internal firm requirement to file within a certain period of time a suspicious or "incident" report when activity appears suspicious. These reports are filed with a central department in firms whereby extensive follow-up and research is done to investigate the matter. After a certain period of time (e.g., 30 days), the matter is either closed as non-suspicious activity or, if the activity does appear to be suspicious, a suspicious activity report is filed with FinCEN.
- Ensuring there is a reasonable and adequate program to identify red flags or indicators of unusual activity and researching such activities and fully documenting the results. Regulators have been critical of red-flag programs that are general in nature and implemented for the purpose of satisfying a requirement rather than being a thoughtful, effective red-flag identification program.
- Being mindful of the enhanced AML risks posed by a firm's involvement in penny-stock transactions—both in executing as well as clearing and settling such transactions. Penny-stock transactions are more prone to fraud—they are more frequently used in pump-and-dump stock manipulation schemes—as well as violations of the securities registration requirements for the sale of securities to the public (e.g., firms have been used by fraudulent parties to sell penny stocks that have not been properly registered with the SEC).
- Being extremely careful in providing market access through your firm—especially in the context of high-frequency trading. If this is a business of the firm, it is extremely important to have the ability to verify the identity of all traders to which the firm provides market access and to have automated and intelligent surveillance systems to detect and prevent manipulative trading activities.
- If your firm transacts with correspondent accounts of foreign financial institutions, ensuring that the firm implements an enhanced due diligence program for this type of account is necessary to ensure the firm is educated on the correspondent bank's business activities and that it has an AML program and customer identification program similar to that required of US banking institutions.
- Ensuring that your AML program investigates and responds to all regulatory inquiries related to potentially suspicious activities or customers.

- Ensuring that the firm conducts a thorough annual independent audit of the AML program, audits it against the type of program that should be implemented in a firm with like business activities and customer base, and that senior management responds reasonably and promptly to exceptions noted in such review.
- Verifying that the data sources utilized for AML surveillance are periodically checked for completeness and accuracy and, if necessary, new or updated data sources are implemented.
- Ensuring the AML program has adequate staffing and resources to address all the risks inherent in the firm's activities.[1]

Registration Department

The compliance department is also responsible for administering the licensing and registration function for the firm and individual employees who may require licensing. Background checks on employees is necessary to ensure an employee has no criminal or regulatory history that would disqualify him from being licensed with a regulatory agency. This could include firm and/or individual licensing with regulatory agencies such as the SEC, FINRA, NYSE, CFTC, NFA, Chicago Mercantile Exchange (CME), Chicago Board of Trade (CBOT), and so on. The primary determination for evaluating the regulator, exchange, market center, alternative trading system (ATS), and so on, where the firm is required to become registered and/or licensed is based on the type of activity that the firm is engaged in and the markets that it wants to access. The supervisory personnel are primarily responsible for understanding their business and communicating this to the registration department of a firm. The registration department is then responsible for communicating to senior business leaders the requirements for registration and licensing of each regulator, exchange, market center, and ATS. The registration department then provides its opinion to the business heads as to which regulators the firm should be licensed with and which business groups may need to be licensed individually. The business heads will then instruct the registration department as to which individuals should be licensed where. The registration department will then execute all firm filings that need to be made to effectuate the firm's approval with the various regulators, exchanges, market centers, ATSs, and so on.

The filings generally request information on the firm, including business address, specific type of licensing being requested, information about senior officers, disclosure of ownership structure, certain affiliate relationships, as well as any criminal, regulatory, or enforcement history. The registration department also works with the specific individuals who will be required to become licensed to complete individual licensing forms that each regulator will require for the individuals to be approved with the respective regulator and in each jurisdiction. This generally includes background information from the individuals—name, address, current employment, employment history for a period of time (e.g., 10 years), and residential history for a period of time—as well as questions on the individual's fitness to be licensed (in the opinion of the venue) such as customer complaint history, criminal arrest and conviction history, any sanctions the individual has received from other regulators (e.g., SEC, FINRA, CFTC), and any history of credit problems.

The individuals need to complete such licensing forms, attest to the accuracy of the information, and, generally, their supervisors will also need to sign or acknowledge in order for the application to be submitted to the regulator.

Regulatory Examinations

The compliance department is also generally responsible for managing the regulatory examination process. This generally includes being the point of contact for regulators during the periodic examinations that occur at capital markets firms.

For example:

- FINRA or the SEC may notify a firm that an examination will be conducted on the firm's sales practices, equity trading activities, and the firm's financial and operational processes and recordkeeping. The regulator will generally inform the firm that they will be on-site at the firm during a period of time (e.g., 45 days from the time of initial notification). The regulator will submit an information request to the firm requesting documents to review prior to coming on-site and to deliver such documents as soon as possible. Generally, it provides a schedule of when it requires each document.

The main point of contact for the regulators in notifying the firm of such examination is the compliance department. The compliance department will also generally be the main point of contact for the receipt and distribution of regulator requests. The regulator will submit a request for information and a due date to the compliance department regulatory examination team and that team will organize and distribute to the various areas to produce such records. The business group will submit such information to the regulatory examination team, who will then forward it to the applicable regulator. If the regulator has questions on the information submitted, such as a firm's business practice, specific questions on a policy, procedure, or written supervisory procedure, or a question on a report submitted, the first line of response would be the compliance department's regulatory examination team. If they cannot answer the question, then they will be the firm's filter by directing the question to the respective businessperson and then communicating any response back to the regulator. If the compliance department believes that intermediating such responses may cause confusion or if the regulator has a large number of questions, then the regulatory examination team may believe a conversation is the best way to resolve the regulator's questions, and they will work to set up a call or meeting between the regulator and the specific business team with the compliance team being the chaperone of such meeting.

Regulatory Inquiries

Regulatory inquiries are another firm responsibility that is handled by the compliance department. Firms that are active in the capital markets arena will receive a number of regulatory inquiries related to their business that will require research (in some instances, substantial amounts of research) and written responses.

For example:

- Firms that engage in equity trading of NASDAQ securities have responsibilities to report the trades that the firm executes to the Automated Conformation of Transactions (ACT) and report order receipt and routing information to the Order Audit Trail System (OATS). Most firms active enough in trading these securities will have issues over time where they may be late in reporting trades or may have inaccurate information in certain trade reports or may fail to report certain trades. This could result from a number of issues, including, but not limited to, late processing of trades by the sales trading or trading teams, systematic issues whereby there is a breakdown in the electronic system the firm utilizes to report its trades that results in late trades, extremely high volume of trades whereby the system is slow due to excessive volume causing trades to be reported late to ACT, or a systematic breakdown whereby trades do not get reported to ACT or OATS. Firms may receive a call from NASDAQ on certain issues and they can be repaired quickly, but many times firms will receive a written inquiry from FINRA or NASDAQ requesting information on the firm's trade reporting deficiencies. Such requests will often seek information such as confirmation that the trades indicated in the letter were either late or not reported, a detailed description of why the trades were late or not reported, any remedial action undertaken by the firm to correct such deficiency, a copy of all the trade tickets and trade confirmations reflecting the specific trades referenced, a copy of the firm's policies, procedures, and written supervisory procedures in place at the time of the trade reporting deficiency, as well as copies of any such documents that were amended as a result of remedial action taken by the firm to correct such deficiency. In addition, firms will generally be requested to provide the names of personnel responsible for reporting such trades as well as the name(s) of individuals responsible for supervising the trade reporting function. Obviously, this is a significant amount of information requested in the regulator's quest to determine the problem, any solutions implemented, as well as any individuals who may have caused the problem. It requires not only a significant amount of documentary information but also coordination with the sales and/or trading departments as well as possibly information technology (IT) personnel and the operations department.

This involves a tremendous amount of coordination among groups to find the root cause of the issue and any solution implemented, whether the firm was aware of the problem prior to receiving the inquiry, and if not, then coordination among these groups to find a solution before responding. Once all the information required to respond is available and provided to the compliance department, the regulatory inquiry team will then draft a written response to the inquiry that will not only respond to the questions posed to the firm, but in many instances provide a persuasive argument as to why the firm should not be referred to the enforcement or legal division of the regulator that determines sanctions and/or fines for firms' deficiencies.

Another example includes:

- Firms may receive inquiries related to their mergers-and-acquisitions business. Regulators review the newswires for public releases of announcements of mergers and/or acquisitions between public companies. FINRA will do so with respect to NASDAQ-traded companies. After reviewing such announcements, a regulator may then review the trading in the stock of such companies prior to the public announcement. If they see anomalies, they may want to confirm that no trading on inside information occurred and as such FINRA may send inquiries to firms involved in those transactions requesting information on how they protected the material non-public information (MNPI) the company received while working on the deal prior to public announcement.

  This type of inquiries comes to the compliance department's regulatory inquiries team as the main contact for the firm. The regulator will request information such as the date the firm first received the MNPI on the transaction, a list of the employees who first received the MNPI, when and to whom those employees shared the MNPI, and continuing until the firm can provide a list of everyone who received such information, the date of their receipt, and with whom they shared such information. If the firm is a global one and the transaction is global in nature, this can cover people all over the world.

In addition, if the regulator does not have access to the personal trading information or accounts of the individuals who have received such information, it will request that the firm provide such information. Obviously, in this situation, the regulator is trying to determine whether the firm handled the MNPI in an appropriate and diligent manner and whether any employee of the firm may have traded securities in her personal account while in possession of MNPI. Assuming no employee engaged in such criminal actions, the regulator wants to know individuals outside the firm with whom the firm may have shared such information. While this outside sharing of information could have been for legitimate purposes (such as for assistance in the merger or acquisition transaction), the regulator would now have the names of additional persons in possession of the MNPI and would request the firm to explain for what purpose it shared such information with people outside of the firm. This could potentially be a massive amount of information that the compliance department must collect as well as then provide a written response to the inquiry in a clear and concise manner. The response must make a persuasive argument that the firm possessed, handled, and shared such information in a diligent and appropriate manner and did not contribute to any mishandling of such information that may have resulted in inappropriate trading in the securities.

Culture

Enforcing a culture of compliance is another important role of the compliance department. While senior management is responsible for implementing a culture stressing the importance of compliance to its business activities and reputation as well as senior management's unwillingness to accept non-compliance with laws, rules, regulations, policies, procedures, and standards of conduct, the compliance department needs to work with senior managers to help them quickly detect and wherever possible prevent activities and/or behavior that violate laws, rules, and regulations. When violative activities or behavior do occur, the compliance department should be a trusted business partner for business heads to seek advice and help escalate issues that need to be brought to the attention of senior managers within the organization.

In addition, the compliance department should work with the business heads to implement corrective action or amended policies, procedures, or compliance programs and/or systems that can help prevent such violative activities or behavior from occurring again. One way for senior managers to enforce the culture of compliance is to include compliance officers on senior management committees, making compliance a prominent voice within the firm. Compliance committee membership may be (and in certain cases should be) in a nonvoting capacity to avoid any appearance of compliance having supervisory authority in a firm's securities or investment banking activities. Participation as a nonvoting member reflects management's view of the importance of including compliance in such meetings as well as documenting in meeting minutes the compliance department's viewpoint on issues before the committee.

Embedding Compliance Officers Within Businesses

Compliance officers may be embedded within certain businesses to be an on-site advisor to the business supervisors. Many firms will include compliance officers trained with certain specific product knowledge to sit directly on trading desks.

For example:

- A compliance officer trained on the rules and regulations of the equity markets, including FINRA, NASDAQ, and NYSE rules and regulations, may be seated on the equity trading and/or sales desk to advise the desk throughout the trading day. In addition, fixed-income, options, futures, and other product-specialized compliance officers may be situated on the respective trading desks to advise firm personnel on the rules and regulations applicable to the various exchanges, market centers, and trading venues.

Another example is dedicated compliance officers for the Volcker Rule:

- Most banks that have trading desks either within the bank or in affiliates will have Volcker Rule compliance personnel advising trading desks. The Volcker Rule, enacted as part of the Dodd-Frank Act, prohibits banks from engaging in proprietary trading of securities, derivatives, commodities, futures, and options on such financial instruments and prohibits banks from owning, sponsoring, or having certain relationships with "covered funds" (i.e., hedge funds and private equity funds). The rule created a number of asset class exemptions as well as certain activity exemptions involving trading with customers such as market making, underwriting, and riskless principal transactions. Each of these requires an analysis of the business activities as it relates to the transactions conducted by the institution. In addition, each of the customer activities exemptions may require considerations of reasonably expected near-term demand (RENTD) and other customer-facing activity calculations. All of this requires a significant amount of advice for how a business must be structured to comply with the Volcker Rule. A compliance officer knowledgeable in the Volcker Rule will generally be embedded with the trading desks to advise as needed.

Coordination

The compliance department may also be the coordinator between the business units and the other control functions such as risk management, internal audit, and other control type groups. During audits—both internal and external—compliance is many times the intermediary in bringing these control groups in contact with and providing information for the various audit teams. In addition, the compliance department will work with various members of the risk management team to ensure compliance and risk are coordinated on risk and control issues. The legal and compliance department will also work together with business units on assessing the legal and regulatory risks the firm may face in its business activities.

Ethics

The compliance department will also be the main enforcer of the firm's ethics program. This program will be composed of certain ethical standards, standards of conduct, and best practices that all employees within a firm are expected to abide by. Many firms implement a code of conduct that outlines the minimum standards of ethical conduct that employees are expected to comply with in order to avoid actual or perceived conflicts of interest between the employee, the firm, and potentially firm customers. Generally, employees will be required to attest to certain matters upon initial employment and annually affirm their compliance with the code. For example, the code of conduct may include, but would not be limited to, the following conduct:

- The employee has not attempted to bribe any foreign government officials in exchange for business opportunities for the company in violation of the Foreign Corrupt Practices Act.
- The employee has not made political contributions for the purpose of influencing an election or in hopes of obtaining business for the company as a result of such donation.

- The employee has not traded on, provided to another without authorization, or otherwise misused MNPI obtained through the firm.
- The employee has not engaged in an inappropriate, intimate relationship with another employee who reports to them, they report to, or is in the same line of supervision.
- The employee has complied with all the policies and procedures of the firm as well as all laws, rules, and regulations applicable to the employee's activities at the firm.

In addition to the code of conduct, the ethics department will also handle issues like providing the firm's permission for employees to engage in certain activities outside of their employment with the firm, such as:

- Employment outside the firm (e.g., a part-time job as a teacher).
- Opening or maintaining brokerage accounts outside of the firm.
- Making political donations (as a donation by certain employees could violate the Municipal Securities Rulemaking Board Rule G-37 on political contributions by municipal finance professionals and municipal advisors).
- Conducting private securities transactions or private investments (to ensure there are no conflicts of interest with the firm's business or customers).

Control Room

The compliance department will also be responsible for implementing an effective control room function. The control room is generally tasked with being the conduit or gatekeeper of all MNPI maintained by the firm. Capital markets firms will invariably receive MNPI from their customers when they engage in activities that necessitate the exchange of such information, such as borrowing money from a financial institution, issuing securities into the private or public markets, or engaging in a merger or acquisition transaction. In these instances, a firm will receive MNPI from its customers engaging in such activities, and the receipt of such information requires the firm to protect it to ensure the firm or its employees do not misuse it. The careless handling of such MNPI by a firm could result in the firm being held liable for insider trading violations under the Securities Exchange Act of 1934.

Depending upon the complexity of a firm's business, it may receive such information from many different customers that engage in activities requiring the exchange of MNPI. The areas of a capital markets firm that receive such information are generally referred to as "private-side" businesses. The areas of a firm that receive or are in possession of only public information and receive no MNPI are generally referred to as "public-side" businesses. The sales and trading areas of securities trading desks are public-side businesses, and it is imperative that those areas do not receive MNPI. The possession of MNPI about an issuer of securities by a trader who trades the securities of that issuer essentially restricts that trader from trading the securities of that issuer. Any trades in such securities by that trader would be while in possession of MNPI.

Even if the trader argued that such information was never utilized in the trade, the mere possession of such information places the burden of proof on the trader to prove such information was not utilized during a trade and being in possession of such information while executing a trade would be an almost impossible burden to overcome. Hence, the trader would most likely be restricted by the firm in trading of such securities until such information becomes public knowledge, and any other trader or salesperson with such information would also be restricted from trading or selling such securities.

The control room needs to identify all of the business areas that possess any such MNPI. In conducting such assessment, firms must do a comprehensive review of businesses that transact private-side business. The following are some capital markets business areas that are likely to possess MNPI:

- *Mergers and acquisitions businesses:* Broker-dealer firms may represent either the sell-side (i.e., a company that is attempting to sell itself, a business it owns, or certain assets) or the buy-side (i.e., a company attempting to buy another company or its assets) and would have MNPI about the company that it represents. Any merger or acquisition transaction will require an in-depth analysis of both companies, and significant MNPI will be shared. If both companies are publicly traded companies and the transaction is viewed as a significant transaction for both companies, then the firm may possess MNPI on both the seller and the buyer. If the merger or acquisition transaction also involves a loan by the firm to one party, or funds for the transaction are raised through an equity or debt securities issuance or a related derivative transaction, then MNPI may need to be shared with other areas of the firm in order to assist on the transaction.
- *Securities syndicate or capital-raising activities:* Corporations periodically will need to raise money through debt or equity issuances or may need to refinance, repurchase, or restructure such issuances. The firm may be a lead underwriter or syndicate member in the structuring, issuance, and distribution of such securities. As part of the due diligence process in such a transaction, a firm will receive MNPI about the issuer that could include earnings from the previous quarter prior to public

release date, adjusted projection of future earnings, business disruption information, and so forth that may not have been released to the public and will not be released until the specific issuance is ready for distribution.

- *Bank loan/loan trading:* Banks (or broker-dealers) may be part of a credit facility that lends money to a corporate issuer through a traditional bank loan rather than a securities issuance. This will involve the banks receiving MNPI about the lender. The lead bank or banks may create a syndicate to distribute the loan and lower their total credit exposure to the loan. The banks will create a loan site for the issuance (which will be the responsibility of one bank referred to as the administrative agent), which will house the MNPI available to syndicate members and other potential investors. While the site will house MNPI, some investors or syndicate members may also trade the securities of the issuer and therefore cannot possess the MNPI, or they will be restricted from trading the securities.

  As a result, such loan sites may have one access for syndicate members and investors who want to access the MNPI and a separate access for those who only want to access the public information on the issuer. This type of situation creates more complications for compliance departments, as they would need a way to verify that loan traders who also trade securities do not access the MNPI on the loan sites of bank loans where they are participants.

- *Credit departments:* The credit department of financial institutions assesses the credit of a party seeking a loan. In such capacity, it will want to see all current information on a borrower. For corporate borrowers that have issued securities that trade in the capital markets, the credit department will require information that neither the general public nor holders of those securities will possess. This information could include lagging earnings, reduced revenue resulting from loss of customers, IRS judgments against the issuer, and other information that may be viewed as material to an investor.

- *Derivative sales departments:* While the derivative sales department of a firm should not have access to MNPI, there may be certain situations where a salesperson has to be brought "over-the-wall" or have MNPI shared with him in order to assist the customer. For example, a customer may need to do a large foreign exchange transaction due to its currency exposure related to a cross-border merger and acquisition transaction, or it may need assistance on an interest rate swap related to a corporate securities issuance that is being done. While the best efforts of all parties involved should be to not share MNPI with the derivative sales and trading group that may restrict them in certain securities transactions, there may be certain transactions where a derivative sales-person or trader must understand the underlying transaction being done that is triggering the derivative trade in order to best assist the customer. Or based on the large size of the derivative, the derivate sales group may be able to assume that there could be no other reason for the counter-party to do such a transaction other than related to a public issuance or corporate finance–related transaction. In those instances, the compliance department may need to make sure the derivative sales group is restricted from trading such issuer's securities until such information becomes public information.

- *Restructuring or bankruptcy restructuring group:* Financial institutions may have groups that specialize in advising companies that require restructurings of debt in order to avoid bankruptcy or advise companies that have already filed for bankruptcy and are seeking advice on restructuring their debt in order to reemerge from bankruptcy to become a financially viable company again. As part of this process, this group may have access to MNPI about the issuer. While the issuer may be in bankruptcy and their securities virtually worthless, this group may receive MNPI about not only the issuer, but also issues that extend beyond the issuer. For example, part of the firm's work with the issuer may disclose that the issuer has extensive debt exposure to another publicly traded company that may not be clear from all public filings. Public knowledge of this information could adversely affect the value of that company. As a result, this information must be considered MNPI and protected by the firm.

- *Public finance:* While there is a limited amount of MNPI involved in public finance transactions, there are situations where a public finance transaction may affect the value of another security and therefore should be treated as MNPI. For example, if a proposed public finance trans-action would refund an outstanding issuance of securities or result in an outstanding issuance of municipal securities being pre-refunded (i.e., its redemption being collateralized by U.S. government securities), then that would result in the public finance team possessing MNPI about the outstanding issuance.

- *Research departments:* While research departments generally only pos-sess public information about the issuers they cover and write research reports about, the initiation of coverage or a change in the price target of an issuer already covered by the research analyst may be MNPI. As a result, firms track and protect the information about such changes to ensure that such information is not released to select investors or outside of the research department before such initiation or price target change is released to the public.

ASSESSING THE EFFECTIVENESS OF THE PROGRAM

The first step in assessing the effectiveness of a compliance program is to understand all of the laws, rules, and regulations applicable to a firm's business. Without performing this initial task, it is impossible to know for certain whether the firm is addressing all its regulatory requirements. Here, the CCO needs to compile, maintain, and update (as necessary) an inventory of laws, rules, and regulations applicable to the firm's business activities and to ensure new or amended laws, rules, and regulations are added to the inventory as they are approved and become effective.

The inventory of applicable laws, rules, and regulations is the starting point for the compliance program. Once completed, the CCO should map all existing firm policies and procedures to this inventory. The purpose of this exercise is to make sure the firm has implemented policies and procedures to address all the relevant laws, rules, and regulations. If there are gaps, then those gaps must be remediated in a timely manner. Next, to ensure there is an effective supervisory process, the CCO should verify that every policy and procedure mapped to the inventory of laws, rules, and regulations has a written supervisory procedure to detail the supervisor's obligations with respect to that policy. In this case, the CCO wants to ensure that there is supervision for all of the policies and procedures applicable to the business. If there are any gaps, these gaps should be remediated in a timely manner with the business supervisors for those businesses.

Next, the CCO will want to do a risk assessment of the laws, rules, and regulations that are applicable to the firm's business. Firms may use various types of systems to rate the risks of the laws, rules, and regulations, but a simplified system may be to review the inventory and apply a three-tier rating system to each law, rule, or regulation of high, medium, or low risk. A firm should define what each of these risk categories means, but another simplified system would be to define laws, rules, or regulations as high risk, where violations by the firm would have a significant effect on customers and/or are matters that would lead to significant regulatory implications such as large fines, censure, and/or a determination by a regulator that such violations are matters requiring immediate attention of the firm to rectify. Medium risk could be those that would have a small impact to customers, and/or regulators may have some concerns and implement small fines or require firms to implement certain amended processes but not as significant as high risk. Low-risk laws, rules, and regulations could be those where violations will have little to no effect on customers, and regulators would mostly likely require firms to amend their processes but not result in fines or censure.

As a result of this risk rating system, the CCO could determine a time schedule for a firm to monitor (and possibly audit) or test a business's policies, procedures, and written supervisory procedures. For example, a CCO may implement a process whereby the monitoring and testing group of compliance uses the aforementioned rating system and those rated high risk are reviewed for monitoring or testing every year, those rated medium risk are tested every two years, and those rated low risk result in monitoring every three years. In addition, the audit department—another independent control function—may also implement a similar system of rating risk and conducting audits. The audit department and monitoring and testing departments normally work collaboratively to ensure they do not engage in duplicative reviews in a year as that would result in wasted resources.

For example, if the audit department has scheduled a review of insider trading one year, then the monitoring and testing department would want to make sure they are not scheduled to conduct a review of the same issue. If the compliance monitoring department collaborates on their schedules with audit and they realize both groups are scheduled for the same review in a year, the compliance and monitoring team may want to adjust their schedule and focus on another high-risk area or an area that has had deficiencies in past years as that may be a more efficient use of resources.

Once the CCO has determined the monitoring schedule, he or she will want to review which laws, rules, and regulations were reviewed in the current year by the monitoring and testing group and see the results of each review to ensure there are no significant deficiencies or, if there are, making certain that they are being addressed with corrective action by the respective supervisor and ensuring that senior management is aware of them. The CCO also wants to make sure that the monitoring plan remains on schedule. For example, each review scheduled for the current year is on plan to be completed, and if any monitoring reviews from the prior year were pushed back to the current year, that they were also completed.

At this point, the CCO has reviewed the inventory of laws, rules, and regulations as well as the monitoring and testing schedules. The CCO can see which laws, rules, and regulations were tested and the results of such testing. In addition, by coordinating with the audit department, the CCO can see the audits that were conducted of laws, rules, and regulations, the results of such testing, and any corrective action necessary and remediation plans to address deficiencies noted in audits.

For those that were not tested by audit and the monitoring testing group, the CCO will want to discuss with other compliance groups—such as the trading desk compliance officers or the compliance department control room—to determine what testing they conducted during the year. Assuming these other compliance departments conducted additional testing, then there should remain a smaller universe of regulations not testing during the year. For any law, rule, or regulation applicable to a business that has not been tested during the year, the CCO would want to make sure that they are on schedule to be tested in the coming years according to their risk rating and they are not behind schedule. For example, if a law, rule, or regulation was not tested during the year, the CCO would want to ensure it was rated as medium or low risk (if utilizing the same sample rating system referenced earlier) and is on schedule for review over the next two years. In addition, the CCO should periodically (e.g., semiannually or annually) review the risk rating system based on the results of audits, monitoring and testing results, testing and surveillance of business compliance officers, supervisor observations, and regulatory inquiries and examinations to ensure that the risk rating system remains accurate or, if certain material deficiencies have come to the attention of the CCO, he or she may want to amend such risk rating to result in more frequent testing by the monitoring and testing group.

SUMMARY OF CCO OBLIGATIONS

It is key to remember that the CCO's obligation is to implement an effective firmwide compliance program to reasonably address the compliance risks faced by the businesses engaged in by the firm. The implementation of an effective program should include, but not necessarily be limited to:

- Identifying the laws, rules, and regulations applicable to the business model.
- Tracking whether the business has policies, procedures, and written supervisory procedures to address such laws, rules, and regulations.
- Implementing a risk-based monitoring and testing system to test the effectiveness of the policies, procedures, and written supervisory procedures.
- Coordinating with other control groups like the audit department to implement an effective, firm-wide testing program (which may include a combination of testing and control groups).
- Verifying that deficiencies identified in the monitoring, audit, or other testing programs are being addressed by the respective business and supervisory groups, or, if there are disputes between the business and control groups, about how an issue should be addressed or whether a noted deficiency is a true deficiency that needs to be addressed, that such issues have been escalated to senior management for implementation or final determination.
- Ensuring that senior management is aware of the compliance risks and issues that need to be addressed and are also aware of the resources that are required to address such risks.

DIFFERENCE BETWEEN COMPLIANCE AND SUPERVISION

As discussed throughout this section, the role of the compliance department is to advise the business on laws, rules, and regulations applicable to the business the firm conducts, assess the effectiveness of policies, procedures, and written supervisory procedures drafted to address such laws, rules, and regulations, conduct monitoring and surveillance of the business (although in some firms' business models surveillance may be a function of the business line supervisors, and compliance simply advises on the surveillance program), conduct training of the business units, and other compliance functions previously described.

The business supervisor's role or the independent supervision function within a firm is responsible for ensuring that the businesses remain in compliance with applicable laws, rules, and regulations and have the authority to direct employees within each business unit to make decisions that will enable the firm to comply with its obligations. The CCO is not a business supervisor. The CCO's only supervisory obligation should be supervising the compliance department and the employees within that department. The CCO role is an advisory one within a control function, and the actions or advice of the compliance department should not be subject to supervisory or business unit approval. While it is very important to have a compliance department that is engaged with the business and willing to provide advice on issues for the various business units, it must be clear to all parties that the role of compliance is advisory and any decisions to be made are those of the business unit and its supervisors and not the compliance department.

If a compliance officer is perceived as having the authority to make business or supervisory decisions, this would exceed the traditional authority of a compliance department and place the compliance officer—and possibly the compliance officer supervisor up to the CCO—in the dangerous position of being viewed as a business line supervisor and, in SEC-regulated broker-dealers, subject to civil liability for failure to supervise a business unit. This is not to infer that a CCO does not have any liability for failure to implement an effective compliance program, but this type of liability is expected by the CCO and occurs less frequently and generally requires a CCO to be negligent in her duties or fail to implement a basic compliance program.

To avoid any form of business line supervisory liability, it is important for the compliance department to make certain their role in the organization is clearly stated. This is where it may be helpful to have a compliance department mission statement to clearly state the role of the compliance department as well as what activities it is responsible for and, just as important, what it is *not* responsible for. In this way, there is no confusion as to the compliance department's role within the organization. It is also very important to make this clear in advisory decisions with the business unit supervisors.

For example:

- It is not uncommon for a sales or trading employee within a trading department to ask his supervisor whether a particular trade can be executed based on certain unique facts. The supervisor may not know the answer, so she may instruct the employee to ask the compliance officer. If the compliance officer is okay with the transaction, then the trader can execute the trade. The trader may approach the compliance officer and ask for advice on the transaction and indicate that he needs compliance approval for the trade. This is where perception and reality may become unclear. It may be unclear whether the supervisor believes the compliance officer must approve the trade in order for it to be executed, or if the supervisor just intended for the trader to ask for the advice of the compliance officer and then gave the trader the authority to make the decision and the trader just interpreted the supervisor's statement as requiring compliance department approval. If the compliance officer responds with a "Yes, it is okay to execute the trade," the trader may believe that the compliance officer has approved the trade. If the advice was incorrect and the trade resulted in regulatory intervention, a regulator will commonly ask the question of who supervised the trade. If this scenario is explained to a regulator, they may understand the facts to be the compliance officer was the approver of the trade, and in this case the compliance officer, supervisor, or CCO could have liability for supervisory failures. This is why it is extremely important for all parties to understand the roles of business supervisors and the compliance department. In this scenario, when a compliance officer is confronted with the trader's question, the clearest response should be to advise the trader on the facts of the trade and make sure the trader understands the regulatory or legal issues involved in the decision. If the compliance officer has some advice, he should make clear to the trader that he is merely providing advice on the scenario and any approval to execute a trade rests with the trader's supervisor and not with the compliance department.

The CCO also needs to be careful to avoid confusion in its role as advisor and not supervisor when the compliance department is represented on governance committees. If the CCO or designee is a member of a committee, it is important to understand the role of that committee. If that committee is making decisions on whether a business transaction should be engaged in or whether a certain business risk should be undertaken by the firm, when the CCO is a voting member of a committee and that committee makes a decision to act, the CCO may be perceived to have been a supervisor or a senior manager and decision maker on that decision, which could subject the CCO to later supervisory liability.

The CCO should be mindful of the decisions involved with each committee where the CCO or designee is a member and whether those decisions are business or transactions decisions, control decisions, employment decisions, and so forth. Where business or transactional decisions are made, the CCO or designee may choose to be a nonvoting member and simply provide advice on the issues presented to avoid any perception that the CCO was a decision maker or supervisor on the issue.

Ted Urban Case

A case that caused a significant amount of concern for compliance and legal officers of broker-dealers was an SEC action brought against Ted Urban, the general counsel and head of compliance for Ferris, Baker Watts, Inc. (FBW), a broker-dealer. Mr. Urban was the general counsel, executive vice-president, and a voting member of the FBW board of directors, the executive committee of the board of directors of FBW, and the Credit Committee. The Legal and Compliance Departments were combined under the supervision of Mr. Urban and he also supervised Human Resources and Audit. In this case, a broker at FBW committed fraud, manipulation, and unauthorized trading in certain customer accounts. Mr. Urban was not the business line supervisor of this individual; however, the SEC found Mr. Urban was a supervisor and charged him with failure to supervise. Factors that contributed to the initial decision were that Mr. Urban's opinions were viewed as authoritative and were generally followed by the business. While he didn't directly supervise the acts of the broker who engaged in this activity, he was a member of the Credit Committee and dealt with issues related to the broker on behalf of the committee.

While the action against Mr. Urban was ultimately dismissed, it was for reasons other than the view that he failed to supervise. That has caused much concern with control groups such as the legal and compliance departments and supports the view that a firm's compliance department must maintain a distinct and clear definition of its role and how it is different from that of a supervisor. Failure to do so can result in unintended consequences and liability.

NOTE

1. K & L Gates, Legal Insight, "12 AML Obligations Every Broker/Dealer Needs to Know," by Jon Eisenberg, Stephen G. Topetzes, Vincente L. Martinez, and Joseph A. Valenti, September 16, 2016.

CHAPTER **5**

Overview: Supervision

Supervision of a firm's business activities and its employees has always been an essential element of securities regulation and remains at the forefront of concerns for securities, commodities, and banking regulators. As a result, the implementation of a supervision framework has become a significant part of any risk management structure in a capital markets environment. Supervision is not solely the responsibility of any single person, department, or group. Firms must implement a culture of compliance and supervision such that all employees charged with supervising or managing any aspect of a firm's business understand the essential importance of adequately supervising both business activities and the individuals charged with carrying out the business lines' objectives. Failure to implement an adequate supervisory structure can have dire consequences for the firm and its supervisory personnel, such that both the firm and individual supervisors can be disciplined or held liable for failure to supervise activities or employees under their supervision.

STRUCTURE OF SUPERVISION

Each firm must determine the supervisory structure to implement that best fits its business model. For the purposes of our discussion, the president, chief executive officer (CEO), or head of a capital markets group is the top-level supervisor (hereafter, the "head supervisor") in a firm. This individual is tasked with determining the supervisory structure that best fits with the firm's business model and risk appetite. There are various supervisory structures that can be implemented. We will discuss three possible structures.

In the first structure, the head supervisor may want to establish an independent supervision structure whereby all business supervisors report to an independent supervisor. The individual in this role is not responsible for revenue generation but is tasked with overseeing and supervising the firm's business activities and the individuals responsible for executing the business plan. The purpose of this supervision model is to have an individual who is not motivated by revenue and can provide an unbiased view of the firm's adherence to all applicable laws, rules and regulations.

The second model moves away from an independent supervisor. In this model, the business head is responsible for the profitability and supervision of their business. The business head reports directly to the head supervisor.

The third model is a hybrid structure whereby the business heads report directly to the head supervisor (as opposed to the independent supervisor model) and each business line supervisor is assigned a supervisory control partner or team. In this structure, the control partners perform a check-and-balance role. They assist the supervisors to satisfy all firm and regulatory requirements, including the implementation of processes, policies, and procedures, training, and testing. They will also work hand in hand with other control partners such as legal, compliance, audit, and risk management to help the business comply with its supervisory obligations.

Once the firm's supervision model has been determined, then each business line must present a supervision plan to the head supervisor. Assuming the plan is approved, the head supervisor will engage, and seek the approval of, applicable firm governance committees. Components of the plan may include determining the number of supervisors within a business, reporting structure, business activities, and associated risks. They must conduct a risk assessment to identify the inherent risks. In addition, they must identify all regulatory obligations inherent in each business and draft written supervisory procedures. These procedures must address how business and its supervisors will satisfy all of their regulatory obligations.

Each designated supervisor is required to attest that they have adequately supervised all business activities and personnel under their supervision. The frequency of such attestation is determined by the firm. While the frequency of the attestation can vary (i.e., daily, weekly, monthly, quarterly), it must cover every day that business is conducted.

In general, securities and commodities rules require supervisors to be qualified and meet standards of training, experience, competence and such other qualifications as required by the regulator. Supervisors in FINRA regulated firms must obtain adequate securities licenses in order to satisfy their supervisory obligations. This is in addition to any prerequisite licensing requirement necessary to conduct specific business activities. Here are some examples of specific supervisory licenses:

> Series 4—Registered Options Principal Examination: Required for supervisory activities of trading, market making, underwriting, and advertising of equity options, foreign currency options, interest rate options, index options, and options on government and mortgage-backed securities

Series 9/10—General Securities Sales Supervisor: Required for supervision of designed general securities sales activities, including corporate securities, rights, warrants, closed-end funds, money market funds, real estate investment trusts (REITs), asset-backed securities, mortgage backed-securities, equity options, mutual funds, variable annuities and variable life insurance, government securities, repos on government securities, municipal securities, municipal fund securities, and direct participation programs

Series 24—General Securities Principal: Required for general securities supervisor's covering activities such as trading, market making, underwriting, and advertising

Series 27—Financial and Operations Principal: Required for supervision of activities including back office operations, preparation and maintenance of a FINRA member firm's books and records, and compliance with financial responsibility rules that apply to self-clearing broker-dealers and market makers

Series 53—Municipal Securities Principal: Required for supervision of municipal securities, including municipal fund securities (e.g., 529 College Savings Plans)

Series 99—Operations Professional Examination: Required for anyone who has management or supervisory authority over certain operational activities, including:

- Client onboarding (customer account data and document maintenance)
- Collection, maintenance, reinvestment (i.e., sweeps), and disbursement of funds
- Receipt and delivery of securities and funds, account transfers
- Bank, custody, depository, and firm account management and reconciliation
- Settlement, fail control, buy-ins, segregation, possession, and control
- Trade confirmation and account statements
- Margin
- Stock loan/securities lending
- Prime brokerage (services to other broker-dealers and financial institutions)
- Approval of pricing models used for valuations
- Financial control, including general ledger and treasury
- Contributing to the process of preparing and filing financial regulatory reports

DELEGATION AND ESCALATION

While delegation of certain supervisory responsibilities is permitted by most regulators and commonplace for large financial institutions, the supervisor who delegates such responsibility remains ultimately responsible for the adequacy of such supervision in the eyes of regulators. A person who delegates any supervisory obligation should require the delegee to attest that they satisfied their requirement.

Each supervisor is responsible for verifying that employees under their supervision are aware of their firm's policy on escalation, the events that trigger escalation, the parties to be notified, and any additional requirements. The type of issue that may require escalation includes reputational risk matters, regulatory issues, customer complaints, and trading losses.

RESPONSIBILITIES OF SUPERVISORS

Each supervisor in a business will have numerous supervisory obligations based on the business activities conducted and the roles of the individuals who are supervised. While there are certain general supervisory obligations that will be common to all supervisors, each business will have certain supervisory obligations that are unique to their activity. For example, there are different supervisory obligations for primary and secondary market activity. Generally, the Securities Act of 1933 regulates primary market issuances (e.g., new issue securities and related disclosure) and the Securities Exchange Act of 1934 regulates secondary markets (e.g., trading and sales practice obligations).

In this next section, we will discuss specific activities related to the supervision of sales and trading businesses.

Obligations of a Trading Supervisor

Trading supervisors' role is complex. They must have technical expertise of the products they trade, markets they trade in, and the applicable rules and regulations that govern their business. Certain activities a trading supervisor is responsible for supervising include:

- *Securities licensing:* The supervisor must be aware of the securities licensing requirements for each activity that is supervised and verify that all traders have the requisite licenses for the business they conduct. For example, a trader in the corporate and government agency securities business will require a Series 7 General Securities Representative Examination license and a Series 63 Uniform Securities Agent State Law Examination license. A trader in the over-the-counter equities market will require a Series 57 Securities Trader Qualification Examination license (instead of the Series 7 license).

- *Understanding the trading strategy of the firm:* Trading desk supervisors must ensure they understand the overall trading strategy of the firm and that traders who report to them understand the firm strategy and are executing trades in line with that strategy.

- *A transactional review of trading activities:* The trading supervisor ensures the trading activity in each trading account accurately reflects the trading activities executed by the firm's traders. The trading supervisor reviews trading accounts, trade blotters, order management systems, as well as relevant reports generated by such systems to ensure traders are engaged in trading activities that reflect the overall trading strategy of the firm. In addition, trading supervisors review reports or have the ability to verify that traders are engaged in activities and products approved by the firm and within the trading and credit limits approved for the specific trading desk or product.

- *Review of trade execution and pricing:* Trading supervisors are responsible for ensuring that traders under their supervision are satisfying their best execution and fair pricing regulatory obligations. For example, if a firm executes a small number of trades, this may be able to be done manually by reviewing all trades. However, think of a trading supervisor who supervises a team of traders that collectively executes 50,000 trades per day. It is impossible to review each of these trades to verify the price that the trader executed at was a best-execution price and a fair price for a customer. The vast majority of firms will do many more trades than an individual could reasonably review manually, so firms need systems and reports that can compare trades executed to the market price at execution and flag or produce a report of exceptions of trades that were not executed at the market price. The trading supervisors then review each best execution or fair pricing exception and address those exceptions.

- *Trading limits, counterparty, and product approvals:* As part of a risk management program, firms implement trading limits to minimize risk exposure. Trading limits may encompass an overall trading limit for the entire trading desks, it may be broken up by product—for example, a separate limit for equity, options, fixed-income, futures, etc—or may be apportioned for a specific desk—for example, corporate bond trading, municipal trading, Treasury bond trading, listed (exchange listed) equities, and listed options—all may have their own trading desk limits. The risk management department will work with the trading desk supervisors to set risk limits. The trading desk supervisor is responsible for making sure the desks remain within its assigned limits. In addition, if there is a need and justifiable reason to exceed a limit, a trading desk supervisor makes sure they are aware of such situations and approach risk management and seek an exception to a limit before a trading limit is exceeded.

In addition to trading limits, some firms have credit risk departments that establish issuer limits. For example, a firm may want to limit its exposure to below-investment-grade credits. Therefore, it may set a limit for a trading desk such that it is only allowed to invest in below-investment-grade credits up to a certain dollar amount. Alternatively, the limit may be to control exposure to certain companies. For example, a limit may be set on the amount of debt issued by Citibank that the trading desk is allowed to hold in position. It is the obligation of the trading desk supervisor to understand the firm's issuer credit limits and supervise the trading desk to ensure they do not exceed such limits.

Counterparty limits are another form of credit limits that a firm may use to minimize its risk. For example, a credit department may assess the counterparty risk of each of the counterparties that the trading desk transacts and implement limits on the amount of exposure a trading desk can have to any single counterparty at any time. The trading desk supervisor must ensure there is a way to monitor such risk and to ensure that each trader supervised does not exceed such limits.

- *Trade reporting:* Firms have obligations to report the trades they execute to the relevant regulator within a certain amount of time from execution. For example, FINRA has TRACE reporting obligations that require firms to report their TRACE-eligible securities within 15 minutes of execution. For equities, FINRA requires trades executed in the NASDAQ market to be reported to ACT within 10 seconds of execution. Other products may have different reporting obligations or regulatory requirements on trade reporting. In addition, reporting obligations exist such as trade comparison with counterparties, repairing or mismatches, and reporting of the entire order audit trail for equity securities. Trade supervisors must be aware of all trading activities under their supervision as well as the trade reporting obligations for the businesses they supervise. They must implement a supervisory program to ensure all trades are executed and reported to the respective regulator within the time period required. In addition, they must have the ability to detect patterns and practices of noncompliance with the trade reporting obligations. This may include systemic issues with trade reporting systems and the noncompliance of individual traders.

Obligations of a Sales Supervisor

Sales supervisors have a unique role. They must have in-depth product and market knowledge, an understanding of their client's needs, and all applicable rules and regulations that govern sales to customers as well as the markets they operate in. Certain activities a sales supervisor is responsible for supervising include:

- *Securities licensing:* The supervisor must be aware of the securities licensing requirements for each activity that is supervised and verify that all salespeople have the requisite licenses for the business they conduct. For example, salespeople selling corporate, equity, and agency securities generally require a Series 7 General Securities Representative Examination license and a Series 63 Uniform Securities Agent State Law Examination license.
- *Approval of new customer accounts:* Ensure that all salespeople under their supervision are aware of the new account opening policies and procedures, which will include the documentation and customer identification requirements for each customer type. When supervising this activity, the supervisor must ensure all salespeople have satisfied the account opening requirements and have sufficient knowledge of the customer and their needs for the supervisor to approve the opening of the new account.
- *Customer suitability:* Supervisors are required to verify that salespeople under their supervision only recommend products and transactions that are suitable for the customer type and in a manner consistent with regulatory suitability requirements and their firm's suitability policy.
- *Communications with the public:* Supervisors must ensure that the salespeople under their supervision are knowledgeable about the rules and regulations applicable to their communications with customers and present such information in a fair and balanced way. Supervisors must implement a reasonable method of supervision to ensure they review and approve applicable client communications (which includes marketing materials, advertising, sales literature, pitch-books, etc.).
- *Customer complaints:* Supervisors must verify that employees under their supervision are aware of the need to disclose all customer complaints pursuant to applicable regulatory requirements and their firm's policy. Supervisors must respond to such customer complaints in a timely manner and escalate to applicable senior managers and/or governance committees.
- *Review of markup/markdown and commission:* Sales supervisors are responsible for ensuring that any markup or markdown or commission charged to a customer is fair and reasonable under the circumstances

and results in a fair price to the customer. Supervision of this activity requires increased focus as markups and markdowns on certain fixed-income securities will become disclosable on customer trade confirmations under a FINRA rule which has not yet been implemented. Specifically, amended FINRA Rule 2232 will require a FINRA member to disclose the amount of markup or markdown it applies to trades with retail customers in corporate or agency debt securities if the member also executes an offsetting principal trade in the same security on the same trading day

Obligations of an Investment Banking Supervisor

Investment banking supervisors must have knowledge in some or all of the following: mergers and acquisitions, buyouts, financial restructuring, public investment banking, and refinancing. In addition, they must have an understanding of their customer's financial needs, capital structure, and an understanding of all applicable rules and regulations. Certain activities that an investment banking supervisor is responsible for include:

- *Securities licensing:* The supervisor must be aware of the securities licensing requirements for each activity that is supervised and verify that all personnel involved in investment banking activities have the requisite securities. For example, individuals involved in investment banking will require a Series 79 Investment Banking Representative Examination license.
- *Governance committee approval:* If a firm is making a commitment on a transaction, such as agreeing to underwrite a certain portion of a new issue or providing financing to a customer, generally, a firm will have a committee review and approve the proposed commitment. The supervisor must ensure that any commitment of the firm is approved according to the firm's governance structure.
- *Due diligence file:* Supervisors must verify that adequate due diligence is performed on each investment banking transaction and that employees under their supervision maintain complete and accurate transaction files.
- *Communications with the public:* Supervisors must ensure that their staff are knowledgeable about the rules and regulations applicable to their communications with customers and present such information in a fair and balanced way. Supervisors must implement a reasonable method of supervision to ensure they review and approve applicable client communications (e.g., pitch-books).

WRITTEN SUPERVISORY PROCEDURES

Firms want a consistent approach to supervision. To ensure that all supervisors understand their roles, responsibilities, and obligations, a comprehensive set of written procedures must be created for supervisors to document the expectations of each supervisory review. A fragmented model creates inconsistencies. For example, if different supervisors reviewing similar or the same activity on a given day use different review methods, their results may be different. One may capture certain substantive information that the other may not. All written procedures should incorporate the following: Purpose of the review, who is preforming the review, frequency, resources used (i.e., systems and reports), procedures to conduct review, how the review will be documented, and escalation procedure for findings.

SAMPLE WRITTEN SUPERVISORY PROCEDURE TEMPLATE

Name of Review: Communications with the public.

Description of what the firm is trying to achieve with the review: Ensure that all communications with the public are consistent with the firm's policies and procedures.

Supervisor conducting review: Head of sales or marketing.

Frequency: Monthly.

Information Resources: e-mail review system or marketing materials, sales literature, advertising.

Procedures: Review that all marketing materials were approved and initialed by a supervisor prior to sending to clients.

Documentation: Sign off on applicable documents.

Escalation: If there is an issue, it should be discussed with the next-level supervisor and senior management.

CHAPTER 6

Central Role of Finance and Operations

Ian J. Combs, Esq.

Financial and operational rules, regulations, and issues play a central role in the risk management and compliance framework of all broker-dealers. The relevant rules in these areas were designed and set forth with two basic goals in mind: To insulate the financial system as a whole and to protect the assets of individual customers from the insolvency of broker-dealers. The regulatory requirements and overall burden are substantially greater for firms that hold customer funds and/or securities; however, all broker-dealers are subject to capital adequacy and customer protection standards. Unlike most business conduct violations, failure to comply with the minimum capital and customer protection requirements on an ongoing basis can result in the suspension of the firm and create the immediate need to raise additional capital or for it to materially curtail its business. Even a temporary lapse can result in the loss of a firm's ability to conduct a general securities business or in other severe restrictions and penalties. Regardless of a broker-dealer's size or complexity, it must allocate the necessary resources to financial and operational areas due to the potential immediate and severe ramifications of noncompliance with the rules.

Like legislation of the 1930s that was the genesis of the first substantial securities regulation in the United States, the financial/operational area of rule-making emerged as a response to a crisis on Wall Street. Near the end of the 1960s, the industry was rattled by several major broker-dealer failures in what is now known as the "paper crisis." Many of these failures were directly related to growth in transaction volumes across the industry, which were increasing as participation in the nation's capital markets grew exponentially. Many back-office processes were manually intensive in this pre-computer era, and firms often became overwhelmed by the sheer volume of pending transactions. This crisis even resulted in the New York Stock Exchange shutting down periodically as a temporary solution to allow its members to catch up with the mountains of paperwork that accumulated.

As broker-dealers became more and more backlogged with pending orders and transactions, some edged toward insolvency. The rapidly increasing transaction volumes contributed to growing complexity of broker-dealers' operations, which ultimately resulted in a lack of adequate oversight. Many firms were unaware of their tenuous financial position due to the pressure and complexity brought by the increasing volumes. The broker-dealers that failed simply lost track of their liquidity and were unable to demonstrate to their customers and counterparties that they would be able pay their obligations and settle all their trades. As some of these firms ran out of cash, customer securities and funds were used in an attempt to save their businesses, ultimately to no avail. When these firms collapsed, they took large amounts of customer assets with them.

The broker-dealer failures that occurred during this era highlighted the inadequacy of capital standards in place at the time. The existing framework resulted in standards that were inherently inconsistent because they varied depending on the exchanges or other self-regulatory organizations (SROs) the firm was a member of. The Securities and Exchange Commission (SEC) felt compelled to act to quell the growing tide of concern and loss of confidence in the nation's capital markets. The SEC's goal was to remedy the inconsistencies through a regulatory regime that created one standard for all broker-dealers, and to impose stronger capital and liquidity requirements than the exchanges and SROs. The SEC also sought to create new rules that required customer funds and securities to be protected and segregated from the firm's own proprietary inventory and cash.

Today, the primary regulatory mechanism to protect customers, counterparties, and creditors from broker-dealer failures is the SEC's "financial responsibility framework." The core elements of this framework consist of the Net Capital Rule (SEA Rule 15c3–1) and Customer Protection Rule (SEA Rule 15c3–3). These two rules work in conjunction to address concerns around the potential failure and insolvency of a broker-dealer. It is important to note that these rules are applicable to broker-dealers only, not their non-broker-dealer affiliates or parent organizations.

THE NET CAPITAL RULE—SEA RULE 15c3–1

The Net Capital Rule in its current form was promulgated by the SEC in 1975 under the authority granted to it by the Securities Exchange Act of 1934. The '34 Act was part of the spate of regulatory legislation prompted by the severe financial crisis and unparalleled economic depression that began in 1929. The SEC maintains that the Net Capital Rule is one of the most important weapons in its arsenal to protect investors because it helps promote the financial viability and public confidence in the securities industry. The Rule accomplishes this by protecting both customers and other financial firms from potential risks by testing the financial strength and liquidity of all broker-dealers. The Rule's liquidity test is to determine if a broker-dealer has sufficient liquid assets to promptly satisfy the claims of customers as well as an additional cushion of liquid assets to cover market and credit risks. The basic idea is that a firm should always be able to liquate in a relatively orderly manner. This is sometimes referred to as the "self-liquation principle," and is a concept that is central to the purpose of the Net Capital Rule.

To determine compliance with the Net Capital Rule, a broker-dealer must perform two computations. First, it must compute its net capital using the methodology prescribed by the Rule. Then, the firm needs to determine its minimum *net capital requirement*, which will vary depending on its business activities. If the broker-dealer's net capital exceeds its minimum requirement, it is likely in compliance with the requirements of the Rule.

Computing Net Capital

A broker-dealer's net capital is calculated by first deducting illiquid assets from ownership equity such as prepaid rents, goodwill, office furniture and equipment, as well as property. The starting ownership equity is required to be calculated under US Generally Accepted Accounting Standards (GAAP) on an accrual basis. These illiquid assets are referred to as "non-allowable assets" and are defined as an asset excluded from the firm's net worth. The Net Capital Rule also provides that essentially all unsecured receivables are "non-allowable assets," with a few notable exceptions such as un-aged commissions and interest accruals. These exceptions and others were carved out in the Rule to provide relief for smaller broker-dealers. After deducting illiquid assets from its ownership equity, the resulting figure is the firm's *tentative net capital*. The idea behind this first step is simple, and was designed to prevent assets that cannot be easily monetized from being included in firms' net capital.

When determining its tentative net capital, a firm must also evaluate its inventory of securities to determine if the positions should be included as allowable assets. Broker-dealers own inventory of securities for various reasons, such as acting as a dealer or market-maker, or holding positions that result from participation in an underwriting syndicate on a firm commitment basis. Inventory positions are reflected at cost as assets on a broker-dealer's balance sheet, but may only be included as allowable assets for the purposes of the net capital computation if they meet certain conditions. As a precondition for the inventory to be considered an allowable asset, the firm must first establish that a security has a "ready market." This means that the security must be able to be sold in a reasonably short time frame. While there is no single factor required to be considered by the Rule, the primary factor is the daily trading volume in the security. The average volumes generally indicate if the market could reasonably support the sale of the entire position. If it cannot be established that a ready market exists, the firm must record the position as a non-allowable asset, thereby excluding it from tentative net capital.

To ascertain a broker-dealer's final net capital, tentative net capital is further reduced by market risk charges referred to as "haircuts." Depending on the type of security, the firm must deduct a certain percentage of the greater of the long or short position in that security to account for market fluctuations. As a general principle, the more prone a security is to market movements, the greater the haircut. For example, an equity security usually requires a 15% haircut while a considerably less risky investment such as a money market security only requires a 2% haircut. The haircuts associated with fixed-income securities vary depending on type and maturity. In general, the longer the maturity of a fixed-income security, the greater the haircut because the probability of default increases over time. As such, short-term US government securities have the lowest charges, followed by municipal and corporate bonds.

After applying the basic deductions to tentative net capital, the firm must consider applying other capital charges for open contractual commitments and concentration. Open contractual commitments generally result from underwriting on a firm commitment basis. In other words, the firm has agreed to underwrite a new issue of debt or equity securities and is contractually committed to purchasing those securities from the issuer. Contractual commitments can also arise from other obligations, including litigation. Concentration refers to the additional risk that resulted when the firm holds a large amount of one security or securities of a single issuer. Where concentration risk is present, additional market risk charges are required because of the large impact that the potential decline in value of that security could have on the broker-dealer.

After applying all the necessary charges, Table 6.1 shows the broker-dealer's net capital.

Minimum Capital Requirements

The second step when evaluating regulatory capital is for a broker-dealer to determine its minimum requirements. The firm's minimum requirements will vary depending on its business activities. The Net Capital Rule establishes absolute minimum requirements ranging from as low as $5,000

TABLE 6.1 Net Capital of the Broker-Dealer

Net Capital	
Ownership Equity	$100,000
Deductions	
Prepaid Rent	($2,500)
Goodwill	($3,000)
Furniture	($5,000)
Equipment	($7,000)
Total	($17,500)
Tentative Net Capital	$82,500
Haircuts	($20,500)
Net Capital	$62,000

up to $250,000. There are various minimum requirements established by the Rule; however, there are two basic types of broker-dealer business models that have the greatest impact on the minimum requirement. These are "introducing" and "carrying/clearing" firm business models.

In general, an introducing broker-dealer only handles various aspects of the relationship with its customers, such as acting as agent for the purchase and sale of securities, and providing investment advice and other account and customer service activities. It does not generally engage in the movement of funds or securities or hold customer funds or securities on behalf of its customers. Due to this, an introducing firm must enter into a clearing arrangement with a carrying and clearing firm for the movement and the custodianship of customer assets. An introducing firm is required to "promptly transmit" customer funds or securities to the clearing firm. This means that if the introducing firm receives funds or securities from a customer, it must transmit them to the clearing firm by 12 p.m. on the day following their receipt. This is also an important customer protection concept that will be discussed later in the chapter.

Introducing firms enter into one of several different types of clearing agreements with a clearing firm. The most common type of clearing agreement takes the form of a "fully introduced" agreement, in which the clearing firm will establish an account for each one of the introducing firm's customers. When this type of agreement is used, the customer usually receives statements directly from the clearing firm and the clearing firm knows the personal information of each individual customer.

Another form of clearing agreement is the "omnibus" agreement. In this form, the clearing firm establishes one account for the introducing firm and does not know the personal information or activity of individual customers of the introducing firm. The introducing firm has the responsibility in this case to prepare customer statements and manage other parts of the clearance process, including margin. Some firms may prefer this type of agreement to protect the trading positions of its underlying customers who are seeking to remain anonymous. Others may choose this type of arrangement to reduce costs by handling many aspects of the clearance process in-house instead of outsourcing them to the clearing firm. Each type of agreement has benefits and disadvantages based on cost, margin treatment, and regulatory burden.

Unlike introducing firms, carrying/clearing firms actually affect the movement of funds and securities related to the purchase and sale of securities. Many larger broker-dealers that are household names are "self-clearing," meaning that they perform all the functions of an introducing and clearing firm. Even firms that do not hold customer funds or securities, but "self-clear," are subject to the highest absolute minimum requirements. This category includes proprietary trading firms that are direct members of clearing organizations such as DTCC, FICC, OCC, or NSCC.

The lowest absolute requirements are for introducing firms (as low as $5,000) while a minimum requirement of $250,000 is set for any clearing firm. These requirements seem low because they are generally insignificant compared with the balance sheet size of many firms. For example, the largest clearing firms have total assets numbering in the hundreds of billions. Fortunately, these are the bare minimum requirements; a firm must choose the higher of these absolute minimums or the result of a calculation based on one of two possible methodologies. The two choices require a calculation to be performed to determine the potential minimum requirement, and the broker-dealer must apply the greater of the balance determined by that calculation or its applicable absolute minimum requirement.

The Net Capital Rule has two methods for computing a minimum net capital requirement, referred to as the basic or alternative methods. The basic method (see Table 6.2) requires that a broker-dealer maintain $1 of equity for every $15 of aggregate indebtedness (or $6\frac{2}{3}\%$ of aggregate indebtedness), whereas the alternative method (see Table 6.3) requires the firm to maintain the greater of $250,000 or 2% of customer-related receivables. Aggregate indebtedness of a firm is essentially all of its liabilities, with the exception of certain adequately collateralized obligations such as repurchase agreements, bank loans, or the secured portion of margin account balances. Customer receivables are generally funds owed by customers to the firm related to the purchase of securities or margin debit balances.

Most small broker-dealers use the basic method because they typically do not hold customer funds or securities and therefore would not be able to apply the alternative method. Large broker-dealers that carry and clear typically select the alternative method because it will usually result in a

TABLE 6.2 Basic Method for Computing Minimum Net Capital Requirement

Basic	
Aggregate Indebtedness (AI)	$360,000
6⅔% of AI	$24,000
Statutory Requirement	$5,000
Minimum Requirement	$24,000

TABLE 6.3 Alternative Method for Computing Minimum Net Capital Requirement

Alternative	
Customer Receivables	$500,000
2% of Customer Receivables	$10,000
Statutory Requirement	$250,000
Minimum Requirement	$250,000

lower requirement. The firm must choose the greater of the absolute minimum requirement or the aggregate indebtedness calculation (see Table 6.2). If the firm is a Futures Commission Merchant (FCM), then it faces a slightly different standard. All FCMs must report as their minimum requirement the greater of $250,000, 2% of customer related receivables, or 4% of customer funds required to be segregated pursuant to the Commodity Exchange Act.

Another important and yet somewhat elusive concept with respect to the Net Capital Rule is the requirement for "moment-to-moment" compliance with its requirements. Pursuant to the rule, a broker-dealer must be in compliance with the Net Capital Rule on a moment-to-moment basis, which essentially can be interpreted to mean "at all times." This sounds simple enough, but the difficulty lies in proving compliance on second-by-second basis. Does this mean that the firm must produce net capital computations continuously throughout the day? The answer is not clear, but it is understood that producing proof of a firm's exact net capital position for every minute of every day is not practical. Most importantly, the SEC and SROs are more concerned with whether the broker-dealer has established a process to effectively monitor its capital position to ensure that it remains in compliance. Most firms also maintain a large cushion of excess net capital that allows for unforeseen fluctuations in their capital and liquidity.

Special Cases—Consolidated Supervised Entities (CSEs)

After facing lobbying pressure from some of the largest broker-dealers, the SEC adopted a major change to the Net Capital Rule in 2004. The change took the form of an exemption to the minimum net capital requirements outlined in the rule whereby broker-dealers with tentative net capital of at least $5 billion would be allowed to apply a different method for computing haircuts. Essentially, this rule change allowed the use of mathematical models rather than the strict haircuts that were previously required on inventory positions. The use of models rather than set haircut percentages reduced the net capital requirements of many large broker-dealers because they were able to demonstrate that some of their market risk was offset by hedges.

After the rule change was implemented, the result was that the largest broker-dealers were able to immediately report higher net capital balances, and were ultimately able to redeploy the newly found excess capital to other parts of their enterprises. In many cases, this excess capital was withdrawn from the broker-dealer altogether. To partially offset the concern created by the loss of capital and liquidity in broker-dealers, the SEC imposed a minimum net capital requirement of $500 million and a tentative net capital requirement of $1 billion for CSE firms.

While these measures were welcomed by the industry at the time of their adoption, this change in policy continues to be controversial. Some observers have commented that it is likely the rule change allowed leverage at firms such as Lehman Brothers and Bear Sterns to increase to unsafe levels. This methodology is still used by a small number of broker-dealers; however, they are the largest and most systemically impactful firms in the industry. Many believe that future rulemaking may seek to address this risk and possibly reverse some of the benefits gained by the industry as a result of the rule change.

Early Warning Levels—Reporting Requirements and Potential Restrictions

The minimum net capital requirements established by the Net Capital Rule are supplemented and enhanced by additional requirements known as "early warning" capital levels. The purpose of these additional requirements is to provide the SEC and SROs with notice that a broker-dealer's capital is falling dangerously low and approaching the minimum requirements. While the SEC receives copies of all notifications of early warning level breaches, it has delegated primary review authority to SROs, such as FINRA.

The SRO responsible for regulating the firm will review each notification and likely require the submission of a plan for the firm to bring capital levels back above early warning thresholds. If the broker-dealer is unable to improve its capital ratios in a timely manner, it may be subject to heightened scrutiny and business restrictions. For example, the SEC and SRO may place the broker-dealer on "alert status," and require it to file supplemental information that allows regulators to more closely monitor the firm's financial health. If a broker-dealer consistently demonstrates that it is not able to improve its capital position or continue as a going concern, the SEC may impose restrictions on engaging in new business, making capital withdrawals, or acquiring new customers.

Early warning requirements are triggered under the basic method if aggregate indebtedness exceeds 1200% of the firm's net capital at any time. Under the alternative method, the warning levels are breached if net capital is less than 5% of customer-related receivables or if net capital falls below 120% of the firm's minimum requirement. If the broker-dealer detects a breach of one of these early warning levels, it is required to notify its SRO and both the regional and head office of the SEC within 24 hours. If an SRO with oversight responsibility determines that a breach occurred and no notification was sent by the firm, that SRO is required by rule to notify the SEC "immediately." Most SROs, including FINRA, have implemented an electronic notification method for these notifications while copies of the notification are still sent by fax to the SEC's regional and head office.

Capital Withdrawals

In an attempt to prevent owners from deliberately placing a broker-dealer in a precipitous financial position, the SEC and FINRA have imposed restrictions and notification requirements around capital withdrawals. With respect to the SEC, basic notification requirements are in place for all firms. Any broker-dealer that withdraws an amount equal to or greater than 20%, but less than 30% of its excess net capital, must notify the SEC and its SRO within two days of effecting the withdrawal. If the withdrawal is equal to or greater than 30%, the firm is required to notify the SEC and its SRO at least two days before the withdrawal is made. The SEC does not restrict withdrawals less than 20% of excess net capital as long as a withdrawal would not cause an early warning level to be breached. While these requirements are applicable to all forms of withdrawals such as cash dividends, loans, or advances to owners, they do not apply to profits or reasonable compensation. These restrictions are also not applicable to withdrawals made for the purposes of making state, local, or federal tax payments.

FINRA members face additional capital withdrawal requirements. Any carrying or clearing member must receive written approval from FINRA in order to withdraw an amount equal to or greater than 10% of its tentative net capital. Generally, approval is forthcoming if the firm is otherwise in a sound financial position and is not experiencing any immediate threat to its liquidity or ability to continue as a going concern. FINRA will usually request some basic information surrounding the proposed withdrawal, such as the purpose (usually withdrawals are made for purpose of paying dividends) and pre- and post-withdrawal net capital projections. The purpose of the review is to ensure customer assets or the overall financial health of the firm will not be adversely impacted by the withdrawal.

FINRA also prevents all member firms from withdrawing capital that was infused less than one year from the date of the withdrawal. This is a measure designed to prevent firms from relying on temporary capital infusions to fund their businesses. For limited purposes, the firm may apply for approval from FINRA to use temporary subordinated loans that are qualified as equity under certain conditions. These limited purposes include underwriting and investment banking deals. Profits, tax payments, and the payment of reasonable compensation are also excluded from these additional FINRA requirements.

FINRA possesses broad authority to restrict a firm's business based on noncompliance with SEC or its own capital adequacy rules when it is a clearing member or holds customer assets. Pursuant to FINRA Rule 4110, a broker-dealer may be required to "restore or increase its net capital or net worth" or face restrictions on all or a portion of its business. The general standard referred to in the Rule is "when necessary for the protection of investors or in the public interest." The authority for such restrictions is documented in FINRA Rule 9557, which states that "FINRA staff may issue a notice directing a member to comply with the provisions of Rule 4110 ... or restrict its business activities, whether by limiting or ceasing to conduct those activities. ...." There is also a procedure outlined in the Rule that allows for an appeal of the restrictions by the member firm.

Assuming no early warning or minimum requirements are breached, capital withdrawals less than 10% for clearing/carrying firms and 20% for non-clearing/carrying firms do not require formal notification or approval from FINRA or the SEC. Despite the lack of a rule violation or early warning breach, the SEC or SRO may request additional information regarding a capital withdrawal during the normal course of surveillance activities. The SEC and SROs perform ongoing financial surveillance of all broker-dealers, which will be discussed further later in the chapter.

LIQUIDITY RISK AND THE NET CAPITAL RULE

During the 2008 financial crisis, many big banks failed or faced insolvency issues due to liquidity issues. Financial institutions are now more than ever examined to determine whether they can meet their debt obligations without realizing great losses. Thus, these firms face substantial compliance issues and conduct in-depth stress tests to ensure they can remain economically stable.

Liquidity Risk

Liquidity risk is defined as the risk that a broker-dealer will be unable to meet its short-term obligations, or essentially pay creditors, counterparties, or customers as those payments become due. What makes liquidity risk such a great concern is that it can destroy an otherwise healthy and profitable business very quickly. Believe it or not, there is not a large degree of liquidity regulation over broker-dealers today. The Net Capital Rule is ostensibly a rule to ensure that broker-dealers have adequate liquidity on-hand; however, it's clear from the recent financial crisis that it may not accomplish this goal. Regulators and industry leaders are not oblivious to the concern around liquidity, and it has been a central focus of both regulators and the financial community to improve liquidity and stress scenario planning.

Liquidity risk management is focused on the potential occurrence of an extraordinary event that would place a strain on the firm's liquidity. It is important to distinguish liquidity stress from a situation where a business is losing money and eventually becomes insolvent. A situation where a business simply fails over time and eventually is forced into bankruptcy is an event that is usually foreseen well in advance and therefore not generally contemplated in liquidity planning.

It is also important to distinguish between capital and liquidity. The concept of liquidity is much different from that of balance sheet capital because a firm's "capital" is a measure of its ownership equity. For most broker-dealers, its capital includes receivables related to financing transactions that will be collected by the firm at some point in the future. Another way to say this is that much of a broker-dealer's capital is made up of nothing but promises to pay or return liquidity at some point in the future. To be sure, the firm usually is holding collateral related to each transaction that is not reflected on the balance sheet; however, the collateral is exposed to market risk and may not be easily or quickly liquidated. It is also possible that much of firm's receivables are unsecured.

When thinking about liquidity, instead of assets and liabilities, it is better to view the balance sheet in terms of sources and uses of liquidity. For example, sources of liquidity are bank loans, secured borrowing, stock loans, and repurchase agreements. Conversely, examples of liquidity uses are firm inventory, customer or counterparty lending, stock borrow transactions, and reverse repurchase agreements. While a little counterintuitive, the key liquidity risk concept is that liabilities are actually sources of liquidity, and therefore liquidity risk is related to assets (non-cash).

In the context of liquidity, non-cash assets are a source of risk because they represent cash the firm does not have on hand and as a result may not have immediate access to. Therefore, the firm can appear to have a strong capital position while lacking the actual liquid cash needed to meet its daily obligations. In fact, both Lehman Brothers and Bear Stearns were well capitalized from the perspective of the Net Capital Rule throughout the financial crises and even as they became insolvent.

There are two types of events that can create a liquidity crisis at a broker-dealer: Marketwide and idiosyncratic. A marketwide event is one where the entire industry is experiencing a panic, such as occurred in 2008. An idiosyncratic event is firm specific, and could consist of any reason for other market participants to be concerned about doing business with that firm. This could be the result of a credit downgrade, news of accounting irregularities, or other negative information about the firm. Either event may create stress on the firm's liquidity. It is important that this risk is mitigated so that a broker-dealer has enough liquidity available to survive such an event. The concept is that with proper planning, a firm should be able to weather a temporary storm.

A good goal is for a firm to be able to survive a period of approximately 30 days while operating in a condition where it is not able to obtain new financing and sales of its assets face steep discounts. The gaps created by a stress scenario can be filled in many ways, including obtaining secured and committed financing facilities as well as term financing transactions, such as repurchase agreements and stock loan transactions. Firms can use a variety of methods to ensure that they are prepared for a significant disruption in their ability to obtain cash.

Anatomy of a Liquidity Crisis

To properly plan for a liquidity stress scenario, the potential cause must be understood. What follows is a brief summary of the events that surrounded the liquidity crisis at Bear Stearns in March 2008. This event marked the beginning of the broader financial crisis that would engulf the financial system later that year. It serves as an example of how quickly events can conspire to generate an irreparable strain on a firm's liquidity.

In early March 2008, the venerable investment bank Bear Stearns was in the midst of a life-or-death struggle for survival. Bear had overextended itself by investing heavily in real estate during the years leading up to the financial crisis. As the financial markets began to convulse, the great profit engine that once produced record earnings and had propelled Bear to competitiveness with its larger rivals was now the very source of its peril. Bear had become a victim of its lust for mortgages and was now vulnerable, weighed down with various toxic assets related to its securitization business.

Bear was only able to sustain itself by borrowing vast sums of money for very short periods of time, usually for only 24 hours. Every morning, Bear's repo desk would need to raise as much as $75 billion so that its obligations for the next day could be met. Raising this sort of cash was an easy task in normal circumstances because Bear would simply dip into its large pool of mortgage-backed and U.S. Treasury securities to use as collateral for the loans. Bear was effectively addicted to this cheap source of funding; its loss or disruption could mean the end of its very business model.

A series of events was about to unfold that would ultimately erode the market's remaining confidence in Bear, leading to the loss of its critical lifeline of short-term funding and ultimately its collapse. Bear opened for business on Monday, March 10, 2008, with approximately $18 billion in cash reserves. The liquidity crisis began to accelerate rapidly for the first time on this day after a major rating agency downgraded one of Bear's largest portfolios of mortgage-backed securities. The market was spooked by the downgrade, causing Bear's stock price to drop by 11% in early trading. Just after 12 p.m. on the same day, one of the firm's largest bank lenders declined to renew $500 million in short-term financing and also terminated a $2 billion credit line. This was a serious indication that the lender no longer considered Bear to be a creditworthy borrower, a sentiment that quickly spread across Wall Street.

In an attempt to quell the growing chorus of concern over the firm's health, Bear released a statement denying that the liquidity rumors were true and that its balance sheet and liquidity positions were strong. It seemed immediately clear that this statement only served to exacerbate concerns. As the financial media pointed out, the mere need for a statement suggested a growing lack of confidence in Bear. Further fueling the environment of fear on this day was a little-known federal banking regulator, the Office of the Comptroller of the Currency (OCC). Although it never officially acknowledged doing so, many reported that the OCC began to call the largest banks to inquire about their exposure to Bear. This greatly exacerbated the panic among Bear's counterparties because no other financial institution was mentioned in the call.

The crisis continued the following day as another major bank lender, ING Financial, terminated its $500 million credit line with Bear. Deciding it was time to step into the fray, the Federal Reserve made a bold announcement in an attempt to calm market fears. The Fed declared that it would make available a facility whereby firms could pledge mortgage-backed securities for short-term financing. Instead of calming markets, it actually stoked fears that the markets were in a critical state of crisis. The Fed's action was perceived as radical, and in fact represented one of most drastic government interventions since the Great Depression.

As a perfect storm of the market's fears overwhelmed Bear, its liquidity evaporated in a very short period of time. More and more counterparties declined to continue short-term financing arrangements, as customers began withdrawing cash and other assets for fear that Bear was on the verge of failure. At the same time Bear was losing its precious sources of liquidity, its lenders began demanding more collateral for its outstanding loans. In the end, Bear was unable to meet these demands and was only able to stave off bankruptcy through a government-assisted acquisition by J.P. Morgan.

Financial Crisis Post-Mortem

The congressional commission convened to determine the causes of the financial crisis later concluded that Bear's failure was primarily caused by its exposure to risky mortgage assets, its reliance on short-term funding, and its high leverage. The commission also found that inadequate supervision by the SEC and its failure to restrict leverage had led to the firm's maintaining insufficient liquidity and ultimately played a major role in Bear's demise.

The SEC was stunned by the speed of Bear's collapse because it remained in full compliance with the Net Capital Rule throughout the duration of its liquidity crisis. The chairman of the SEC at time of Bear's collapse testified before Congress that Bear had a net capital cushion well above what is required during the entire week leading up to its collapse, and even at the time of its insolvency. The collapse of Lehman Brothers followed a similar pattern where the confidence of customers, creditors, and counterparties quickly eroded, resulting in the loss of critical financing sources. Both of these institutions were well capitalized through the lens of the Net Capital Rule, but ultimately failed due to a lack of liquidity. It is clear that the Net Capital Rule was not effective in these instances because it did not adequately identify and mitigate liquidity risk. As a result, many feel that the current regulatory framework is built on an inadequate foundation because many firms appear sound while they are in fact exposed to a severe degree of risk.

Potential Rule Making

A perceived flaw of the Net Capital Rule is its failure to account for maturity transformation risk. While it properly considers asset liquidity through the application of market risk ("haircuts") and other deductions, it does not consider the relative maturity of a broker-dealer's assets and liabilities.

The difference in the maturity of broker-dealer's loans and its borrowings is sometimes referred to as a funding tail, or mismatch. The source of liquidity risk from a funding tail is present when the firm relies on short-term sources of cash to finance the longer term lending activity. If these short-term sources of funding disappear, the firm may be unable to finance its business if the funding tail is greater than its other contingent sources of liquidity.

Many broker-dealers finance their business through secured financing transactions like repurchase agreements. In a repurchase agreement, a firm will usually post collateral in the form of US Treasury or Agency Mortgage-backed Securities in exchange for cash. Repurchase agreements can take the form of "open" or "term." Open contracts are transactions that have no fixed end-date, but can be terminated within 24 hours, meaning that the firm must return the borrowed cash to the lender the next day. Term transactions may last for any period greater than one day, and sometimes have termination dates month or even years later. Bear's chosen method of financing its daily liquidity was through "open" repurchase agreements, because it was the most cost-effective, or cheapest, way to fund its business.

The problem arises when this type of financing is no longer available because of some event. While most repurchase counterparties "roll" or choose to enter into another short-term loan every day for many consecutive days in a row, there is no obligation to do so past the 24-hour period. As a result, if the broker-dealer has no other sources of cash, it will likely quickly become insolvent if it is overly reliant on short-term funding. A way to mitigate this risk is to reduce the funding tail or mismatch by relying on longer-term financing. In this example, Bear could have reduced the amount of cash it needed to raise every day by entering into term-repurchase agreements.

Another type of strategy that may implicate a high degree of liquidity risk is where a firm operates a proprietary trading strategy that requires it to hold large amounts of inventory that is financed through margin or repurchase agreements. A firm like this would face margin calls from its lenders if the value of its inventory declined, meaning that it would need to provide additional cash or collateral for its outstanding loans. A firm that is highly leveraged may not have enough liquidity on hand to meet these margin calls, resulting in a state of default and insolvency. This particular issue played a major role in the failure of the large commodities-based firm MF Global. The firm made massive bets on Europe by purchasing the sovereign debt of some of the most unstable countries and using the securities as collateral to obtain financing. As the sovereign debt crisis began to take hold in Europe, the value of the collateral that MF Global posted for these transactions declined dramatically, resulting in margin calls from the firm's lenders.

MF Global simply was not able to meet these margin calls as its pool of available liquidity dried up.

Due to the Net Capital Rule's perceived inability to effectively expose and curtail liquidity risk at some financial institutions that have a high degree of liquidity risk, a more flexible regime may be proposed and subsequently adopted.

Special Considerations for Bank-Owned/Affiliated Broker-Dealers

While the liquidity of stand-alone broker-dealers is regulated by federal securities laws and regulations, broker-dealers that are owned by bank-holding companies are subject to more stringent standards. In addition to securities regulators, bank-owned broker-dealers are indirectly regulated by the Federal Reserve and other US banking regulators. Furthermore, a broker-dealer owned by a foreign bank may be subject to the requirements of foreign banking regulators. While the compliance and finance departments of the broker-dealer may not be focused on these additional requirements, the banking liquidity regulations will certainly impact the broker-dealer's behavior and limit the use of its balance sheet and available liquidity.

One such requirement that has become an industry standard is the Basel Committee's Liquidity Coverage Ratio. Essentially, it requires that the entity have enough high-quality liquid assets that would allow it to survive a period of 30 days during a stress scenario. While the Basel Committee's standards are imposed upon most European bank-holding companies, the Federal Reserve has adopted similar standards, which are viewed by many as even more stringent than those recommended by the Basel Committee. There are minor differences in approaches, but the basic concept of the LCR is the same under both regulatory regimes.

U.S.-regulated bank-holding companies are also subject to the Federal Reserve's Comprehensive Capital Analysis and Review program (CCAR). The Federal Reserve describes CCAR as "an annual exercise by the Federal Reserve to assess whether the largest bank-holding companies operating in the United States have sufficient capital to continue operations throughout times of economic and financial stress and that they have robust, forward-looking capital-planning processes that account for their unique risks." This process is mandatory and gives the Federal Reserve the authority to reject a firm's capital plans and require changes to capital levels. It is important to note that each plan is unique and is based on the business model of the firm in question.

The Federal Reserve has also implemented an additional process for firms that are identified as systemically important. These institutions currently consist of 14 of the largest financial institutions in the United States. Systemically important entities are subject to the Federal Reserve's Comprehensive Liquidity Assessment and Review program. Like CCAR, this process is tailored to review and assess each firm's preparedness to deal with a liquidity crisis based on its own unique risks. The program takes a more in-depth look at the entity's asset portfolios, balance sheet, and stress planning.

THE CUSTOMER PROTECTION RULE—SEA RULE 15c3-3

Another outgrowth of the paper crisis of the late 1960s was the Customer Protection Rule as well as the Securities Investor Protection Act, which established the Securities Investor Protection Corporation (SIPC). Customers had collectively lost over $100 million in assets as a result of the many broker-dealer failures that occurred during 1960s. The grievous customer losses included securities that were fully paid for by customers, and even customer cash balances that were not encumbered by any liability to the broker-dealer. As broker-dealers ran into financial difficulties, some had resorted to the use of customer funds and securities to finance their business operations. The conversion of customer funds and securities greatly exacerbated these customer losses.

It was clear to Congress and the SEC that action was needed to prevent customer losses in the event of broker-dealer failures. Congress looked to another time of financial crisis in America for a solution to the growing crisis of confidence premating the financial markets. During the Great Depression of 1930s, the Federal Deposit Insurance Corporation (FDIC) was created to restore confidence in the nation's banks. It was hoped that a similar safety net for the securities industry would reaffirm the faith of the investing public in broker-dealers and the financial system as a whole. SIPC was Congress's attempt to replicate the success of the FDIC, along with the creation of the Customer Protection Rule. SIPC protection today covers customer losses up to $500,000 for securities, and cash balances with a cap of $250,000. While SIPC liquidations do occur, they are rare thanks to the Customer Protection Rule. That is, the SIPC general fund is rarely needed because most broker-dealers who fail are able to quickly return customer assets due to the Customer Protection Rule.

Possession or Control

Adopted in 1972, the Customer Protection Rule has two critical concepts that work together to ensure that customer assets are protected in the event of a broker-dealer's insolvency. First, the Rule requires that the broker-dealers maintain physical "possession or control" of customers' fully paid and excess margin securities. The intent of this aspect of the Rule is to ensure that securities can be returned to the customer on a timely basis following the insolvency of a broker-dealer. This requirement includes both fully paid for securities and excess margin securities. "Fully paid" securities are simply securities that a customer has paid for in full, and has no outstanding liability to the broker-dealer for the purchase of those or other securities. In the industry, these types of transactions occur in what are referred to as "cash accounts," or accounts where every purchase must be fully paid for upon settlement. The other predominant type of account is what is referred to as a margin account. In a margin account, customers may borrow the funds to purchase securities. The restrictions and requirements around the extension of margin are governed by FINRA, SEC, and Federal Reserve rules and regulations.

For the purposes of the Customer Protection Rule, "excess margin securities" are those which exceed the value of securities the firm is able to use to finance customer borrowing. Essentially, excess margin securities are securities that are not being used as collateral by the customer for a margin loan. In this respect, the Customer Protection Rule grants relief for broker-dealers by allowing the use of customer securities to finance margin loans. However, by requiring excess margin securities to be protected, the Rule ensures that securities not being used by the customer for financing purposes are treated like fully paid securities. The use of customer assets is limited by the Rule, but their use was intended to facilitate and promote customer lending throughout the industry. Without the ability to use some customer assets to finance customer borrowing, broker-dealers would find customer financing activity not economically viable.

The core section of the Customer Protect Rule is SEA Rule 15c3–3(b)(1). This Rule states that "a broker or dealer shall promptly obtain and shall thereafter maintain the physical possession or control of all fully-paid securities and excess margin securities carried by a broker or dealer for the account of customers." The Rule defines a customer as "any person for whom or on whose behalf a broker-dealer has received, acquired or holds fund or securities." The important distinction with respect to the definition of *customer* under the rule is between other broker-dealers and natural persons or other non-broker-dealer corporate entities. Essentially any non-broker-dealer entities are considered "customers" for the purposes of this Rule. Non-broker-dealer corporate entities, including hedge funds, are considered customers even though they are institutional entities. The proprietary assets of broker-dealers are also protected in a similar way; however, this is part of a separate reserve computation with different rules and standards.

There are several important exceptions to the definition of *customer* under the Rule besides other broker-dealers. Any natural person or corporate entity that is a general partner or a person who acts as a director or principal officer of the broker-dealer is considered a non-customer under the Rule. These generally include the president, treasurer, secretary, or any person who is performing a similar function. These exceptions exist to prevent these individuals from benefiting from the protection of the Rule. Officers and directors have an obligation to their customers and should not be able to have priority in a scenario where their actions caused the firm to be liquidated and customers have not yet been made whole.

Another important concept to understand is how the Rule views "possession or control." Possession is generally defined as securities held in the firm's physical possession. An example of physical possession is securities held in a vault. Control refers to those securities that are held by a third party on behalf of the broker-dealer. In order to be considered a good "control" location, these securities must be able to be obtained by the broker-dealer without payment of money or other form of value. Essentially, the securities must be held free of any liens or other claims. The most common control locations in modern times are clearing corporations, depositories, or other clearing firms. Other good control locations can include foreign depositories; however, they must be reported to and approved by the SEC.

All fully paid and excess margin securities must be segregated from the firm's proprietary inventory and marginable customer securities. This involves clear notations on the firm's books and records that these securities are segregated for the purposes of the Customer Protection Rule. The Rule also requires safeguards to ensure that securities will not be sent by the firm if it would result in the amount of securities in its possession or control to fall below the minimum requirement. Today, many of the firms that hold large amounts of customer securities employ various automated systems to assist with this process. The notation will clearly appear on the firm's stock record, which is sometimes referred to as the firm's "bible" due to its importance. A broker-dealer's stock record contains a listing of all the securities held by the firm, both on behalf of its customers and its own proprietary inventory.

When working correctly, the firm's controls will prevent its segregated securities from being released for delivery as part of a firm's sale or financing transaction. Preventing the release of segregated securities ensures that the firm always has on hand enough of a particular issue of security to return a customer's fully paid or excess margin securities.

The Reserve Formula

The mechanism used to protect customer cash balances or "free credits" and other customer payables that are not fully paid securities is the customer reserve formula. Following a methodology prescribed by the Rule, the firm is able to determine the amount of customer assets it needs to protect at any given time. The firm determines its reserve requirement and thus ensures that it has enough cash or qualified securities in a special reserve account to make customers whole quickly in the event of liquidation.

A broker-dealer may establish more than one reserve account and could use either cash or qualified securities to fund it. "Qualified securities" are only the very most secure investments that are not subject to a high degree of market risk, such as US Treasury securities. The Rule sets certain conditions for the reserve account, the most important of which is that the account be free of any liens or cross-claims. In effect, this account must be separate from the firm's other accounts, such as its operating or clearance accounts. To achieve this distinction, the account must be expressly titled "Special Reserve Account for the Benefit of Customers," and the bank must provide a letter to the broker-dealer that states the account is not subject to any liens or cross-claims. The overarching principle is to ensure that the funds deposited in the reserve account are quickly and freely accessible in the event the broker-dealer becomes insolvent. Balances in the firm's other accounts will likely become the subject of a long and drawn-out bankruptcy process. Other types of firm accounts will be subject to the bankruptcy process, such as its operating and proprietary investment accounts. The reserve account is also subject to other restrictions, including limitations on the amount of reserve funds that can be placed at an affiliate bank.

Reserve computations are generally performed weekly, which is the minimum frequency required by the Rule for most firms. Some broker-dealers choose to conduct reserve computations on a daily basis. Daily computations may help some firms in managing their liquidity. This is because a broker-dealer's requirement will fluctuate during the week as customers buy and sell securities, or deposit and withdraw cash. The Rule also requires that each broker-dealer perform a month-end reserve computation. A small number of broker-dealers perform computations only monthly; however, these are firms that generate very few customer payables and operate under strict guidelines. Firm's that are exempt from the requirements of the Customer Protection Rule, such as introducing firms, do not conduct any reserve computation. The various exemptive provisions of Rule will be discussed later in the chapter.

Weekly reserve computations are conducted on Mondays as of the close-of-business of the following Friday. After computing its reserve requirement, the firm has until the following morning (Tuesday) at 10 a.m. to make any required deposit. The firm may also make a withdrawal if it determines it has excess funds. Any deposit or withdrawal made after the deadline will result in a rule violation. For example, if the firm determines it has a requirement of $100,000, and only has $80,000 in its reserve account, it must make a deposit of at least $20,000 prior to 10 a.m. the following day. Failure to do so would result in a reserve deficiency of $20,000. Technically, if the deposit was made at 10:01 a.m., a reserve deficiency would exist for that one minute. While this seems immaterial, it should be noted that the broker-dealer must promptly report the deficiency to its SRO and the SEC. In addition, please note that a holiday that falls on a Monday or Tuesday will modify the deadline.

The reserve formula itself can be complex depending on a broker-dealer's business and overall size. To simplify, the broker-dealer's reserve requirement is equal to customer credits less customer debits. This means that the firm adds up all its customer payables and subtracts the aggregate amount of margin loans and other customer receivables. At its most basic level, this tells the firm the net amount of customer obligations it would have in the event of liquidation at the time the computation is performed. If the broker-dealer determines it has more customer credits than debits, it has a reserve requirement. Conversely, if customer debit balances exceed customer credits, then it does not have any reserve requirement. Customer fully paid and excess margin securities are not included in the reserve computation because they must be in the firm's possession or in a qualified depository or clearing firm. The reserve formula is meant to cover cash payables to customers only. Customers' unencumbered assets need only be held in a safe place separate from the firm's proprietary inventory, so that they can be quickly returned in the event of insolvency.

Many firms use a system of determining which credit and debit items need to be included in the reserve formula computation referred to as an "allocation." The allocation system draws information from the firm's stock record. A good rule to remember when considering whether a credit needs to be included in the reserve formula is that all customer liabilities are always included. This, of course, is the whole point of the reserve formula: To protect customer liabilities. Credit items that need to be considered are bank loans, short positions, fails-to-receive, and securities loaned. Debit items, or customer obligations to the broker-dealer that are subject to the allocation process, include long positions, securities borrowed, and fails-to-deliver. These items are defined as follows:

- *Bank loans:* These are loans obtained by the broker-dealer to finance its customer lending activity that are collateralized by customer securities. If customer securities are not fully paid or excess margin securities, they may be pledged as collateral for a bank loan. While this might be a good way to finance its customer lending business, use of these funds to finance the firm's day-to-day expenses is not economically viable.

This is because the firm will need to deposit in its reserve account the full amount of the loan that is collateralized by customer securities. Unsecured or bank loans collateralized by proprietary inventory are not included in the reserve formula.

■ *Long/short positions:* Customer long positions must be included as credit items in the reserve formula while customer short positions act as an offsetting debit item. Proprietary and non-customer positions are generally not included in the reserve formula.

■ *Fails-to-receive/deliver:* A fail-to-receive is a liability of the firm and generally results from payment not being made by a counterparty or customer related to the purchase of securities. If payment is not received past settlement day, a fail occurs. A fail-to-deliver is a firm receivable that results from the broker-dealer having not delivered out securities that it sold, usually because it has not received payment for the sold securities after settlement day. Customer fails-to-receive must be included in the reserve formula, but may be offset by corresponding customer fails-to-deliver. Often, a broker-dealer is just an intermediary between two customers; therefore, it will have offsetting debits and credits when a securities transaction does not settle in a normal time frame for any reason.

■ *Securities borrowed/loaned:* Broker-dealers may conduct financing activities for several reasons; however, one of the most common reasons is to accommodate customer short sales or finance their margin activities. Therefore, a stock loan transaction that is collateralized by customer securities must be included as a credit in the reserve formula. Partially offsetting the credits are corresponding stock borrow transactions that are included in the reserve formula as debit items.

■ *Suspense items:* Operational issues create temporary "breaks" or unreconciled differences that require further investigation by the firm before their source can be identified. For firms that carry customer accounts, these unreconciled differences must be included as credits in the reserve formula. This is because there is the potential that they are related to customer payables, since the firm can't determine what they are related to. An added benefit of this aspect of the rule is to provide an incentive for firms to have an effective process in place to monitor, track, and prevent operational issues.

Utilizing an allocation system allows a broker-dealer to easily separate transactions that are customer and non-customer related. The objective is to ensure that the broker-dealer does not waste resources by reserving or protecting proprietary or non-customer-related transactions. Each firm will tailor its allocation hierarchy based on its business model. Some small firms will use very simple allocation methodologies while larger firms will choose more complex methods in an attempt to attain maximum efficiency. While the broker-dealer has freedom to design its own allocation, regulators require that a consistent approach is adopted. This means that it is not permissible for the broker-dealer to continually change its allocation to seek benefits. It has been determined that constant changes would expose the broker-dealer to the potential for miscalculation as well as operational issues and ultimately place customer assets at risk.

The Reserve Formula and Liquidity Risk—"The Death Spiral"

The reserve formula and resulting deposit requirement have a unique impact on the firm's liquidity. As stated previously, the use of customer securities for financing creates a reserve requirement, but this burden is reduced by a corresponding debit item when the firm is facilitating customer lending. No such benefit is available when the broker-dealer uses customer securities for the purpose of financing its day-to-day operations. For example, if the firm posts customer excess margin securities for a bank loan of $100 million on Monday, it will need to fund an additional reserve requirement of $100 million after it performs the next reserve computation. If the firm needs to use customer securities to fund its day-to-day operations (outside of customer financing), then it is likely in financial difficulty. As it takes out more and more loans using customer securities as collateral, it continues to exponentially increase its reserve requirement. This will drain the firm's available liquidity until it's completely gone. It is therefore important to understand the interplay between the reserve formula and the liquidity profile of the broker-dealer. This is known as a spiral condition and is something that is closely monitored for by regulators.

Exemptions from the Customer Protection Rule

There are several exemption provisions from the Customer Protection Rule, which are available to firms that do not hold customer funds or securities. The most common is the exemption contained in paragraph k(2)(ii) for introducing firms that clear all customer transactions on a fully disclosed basis to a clearing firm. The next most commonly claimed exemption is contained in paragraph k(2)(i), which is generally claimed by firms that may have payables to customers who are trading on a delivery-versus-payment/receipt-versus-payment basis. In this capacity, the firm must effect all transactions involving customer funds through a special reserve account. Another commonly claimed exemption is for those firms that have a business limited to only acting as agent for customers who purchase subscription way securities. These types of products include mutual funds and insurance products, such as variable annuities.

No matter which exemption a broker-dealer is operating under, it must promptly transmit all customer funds or securities to a clearing firm or an issuer. The SEC has defined *promptly transmit* to mean that the funds or securities must be forwarded to the clearing firm by noon of the first business day following the date they were received. While the requirement to promptly transmit customer funds and securities has been interpreted narrowly by the SEC, there are three scenarios for which the SEC has granted relief. All of these scenarios allow additional time for the purpose of facilitating a review and/or approval that is required by rule.

PREPARATION AND REPORTING REQUIREMENTS

Each broker-dealer must have a licensed financial/operational principal to oversee the preparation of the net capital and reserve computations as well as any other financial/operational reports the firm is required to produce. This individual is also responsible for ensuring the firm makes the required notifications to the SEC and/or its relevant SRO, which is FINRA for most broker-dealers. Generally, the preparation and reporting functions are housed within a department called Regulatory Reporting. Alternatively, these activities may be part of the firm's finance or accounting departments. The smallest broker-dealers may only have the Financial and Operational Principal (FinOp) involved in this function, who in most cases is also the CFO or is acting in multiple capacities at the firm. Regardless of its size and complexity, each broker-dealer is expected to establish and implement policies, procedures, and controls that are reasonably designed to ensure compliance with the applicable rules. To this end, it must have an infrastructure in place that is adequate. The larger and more complex firms will often have many people participating in the production of this reporting.

The mode of reporting this information to the SEC and SROs is through a form filing known as the Financial and Operational Combined Uniform Single or "FOCUS Report." Today, this filing is made electronically through a platform maintained by FINRA known as efocus. Most firms are required to file the FOCUS report on a monthly basis, although some small firms with limited business models are only required to file quarterly. The standard FOCUS report contains not only the Net Capital and Reserve Computation, but also the firm's balance sheet and other supplemental information. The FOCUS balance sheet is a standardized template to promote uniformity in the reporting of balance sheet items. There are two basic types of FOCUS reports, one for clearing firms and another for firms that are introducing only. The clearing firm's FOCUS report (FOCUS Part II) includes more information while the introducing-only report (FOCUS Part IIa) is far more limited.

In addition, depending on business activities, most broker-dealers will likely be required to file other forms and schedules to supplement the information captured in the FOCUS report. Most FINRA member firms with inventory are required to file Form Supplemental Inventory Schedule, which provides a more detailed view of the firm's inventory. All FINRA members are also required to file the Supplemental Statement of Income, or Form SSOI, on a quarterly basis. This filing provides a very detailed picture of the income statement and gives regulators and unprecedented look into a broker-dealer's business. There are also schedules to capture information regarding off-balance-sheet items (Form OBS) and custodial locations (Form Custody). Other SROs and FINRA may require any broker-dealer to file additional reports or information as needed to conduct financial surveillance.

Pursuant to SEC rules, every broker-dealer is also required to have an annual audit of its financial statements conducted and reported to the SEC and its SRO. The broker-dealer's annual audit is a standard corporate accounting audit with some additional requirements. The audit report must contain a Net Capital Computation and reconciliation of any differences between the auditor's computation and the FOCUS report filed as of the firm's fiscal year-end. The audit report must also contain a reserve formula computation and a statement that there are no material differences between auditors' reserve computation and that reported in the fiscal year-end FOCUS report. To the extent material differences are identified, the auditor must provide a reconciliation of those differences and an explanation for each. In general, SROs or the SEC will verify that the auditors' finding align with the information disseminated in the FOCUS report.

The audit must also include a statement that the firm's controls over its compliance with the Customer Protection Rule were effective during the audit period, which is an entire fiscal year. If the firm does not regularly hold customer funds or securities, the audit may include an exemption report. The exemption report will simply state that the firm was in compliance with its exemptions from the requirements of the customer protection rule during the period. This is a relatively new requirement created in 2015 with the SEC's sweeping revisions to the financial responsibility rules.

OPERATIONAL RISK

Operational risk can be defined in several different ways. It is important to distinguish between the risk as it relates to the firm's operations department specifically and operational risk generally. In its broadest sense, operational risk can be present in any area of the broker-dealer. For the purposes of this discussion, operational risk is best defined as the potential for risk associated with a broker-dealer's people, processes, and technology. It's obvious from this definition that operational risk is an inherently broad category and as a result it can be difficult to assess. Operational risk is also one of the few risk areas that directly impacts all others. This means that operational issues can enhance or exacerbate the other risks at the firm. Regardless of the difficulty posed by operational risk, its importance cannot be understated.

Broker-dealers primarily manage operational risk across four areas:

1. *Business lines—front office:* While the business areas are focused on producing revenues, they also represent the front line of defense and are in the best position to prevent operational risk before it becomes an issue. Generally, business lines are responsible for the first level of review, monitoring, and approval policies and procedures designed to mitigate operational risk. The business areas essentially provide a self-contained control function that acts somewhat independently of the compliance and other control functions. It should be noted that the inherent tension between the desire to earn revenues and the need to prevent operational problems may render the controls of this area as less effective. To be sure, the front office shares the same interest in preventing operational issues with compliance; however, the expertise and incentives within the business units may make their controls less effective.

2. *Compliance and legal:* The compliance and legal functions represent the second line of defense and first true independent control function. This area is responsible for several important functions. First, these groups must ensure that new rules and regulations are considered by the business. In most cases, this will involve the development and implementation of new policies and procedures designed to comply with new rules. Compliance and legal will also conduct independent monitoring and testing of the business areas.

3. *Middle/back office:* This area of the firm conducts a large degree of the monitoring and reporting of transactions and other critical information. This area generally produces regulatory reports and financial analysis that ensure the firm remains in compliance with the applicable capital and customer protection rules. It is important that this function has the necessary processes and procedures in place to monitor the firm's financial position and communicate with the business areas. This must be an area of focus especially for a clearing firm, due to the potential for operational issues in the back office to place the firm in financial peril.

4. *Technology/systems:* A firm's systems and technology support staff play a critical role in the firm's operations. A robust testing regime and governance structure should be established to prevent operational issues.

The firm will also need to have the necessary infrastructure to be able to quickly identify and resolve system issues. The importance of this function cannot be understated. Consider the recent example of Knight Capital Markets. This firm was a market maker on the New York Stock Exchange and played a central role in the US equities markets by acting as an intermediary between buyers and sellers. Knight's technology staff made a routine update to its trading systems and made the simple mistake of failing to copy the new code to all of its servers. Knight did not have a testing program that was able to identify the error before the change was implemented. The next day after the update was made, Knight's trading systems began to act erratically and began selling and purchasing securities uncontrollably for a period of approximately 45 minutes. By the time the firm was able to identify the issue and shut the system down, the damage had already been done. This issue created losses reaching into the hundreds of millions and ultimately led to the firm's failure.

5. *Internal/external audit:* The third line of defense is the firm's internal audit program as well as the external audit function. These groups act as a further independent check on of all the control functions at the firm. A good internal audit program will be targeted based on risk.

Other Considerations

A firm's culture of compliance may impact the level of operational risk present due to its impact on the people who work there. In other words, cultural values at a broker-dealer may drive business conduct. Values and culture are not necessarily easy aspects of an organization to manage. However, firms can set ethical standards and create an environment where harmful behaviors are not tolerated. Training programs, proper supervision, and compensation programs designed to create incentives for behaviors that are in line with the firm's values can be implemented to mitigate this risk.

Another potential operational risk is derived from a firm's outsourcing and vendor relationships. Not only do these relationships need to be properly vetted, but critical relationships should be monitored on an ongoing basis. The same considerations apply to any new business relationship or product offering. Firms should have a robust governance framework and written policies and procedures to govern these processes.

Supporting operational activities with inadequate tools can also greatly increase operational risk. Firms need to have the right systems and resources to be able to effectively execute their operational functions and regulatory obligations. For example, overly manual processes tend to be error prone, and may not be appropriate for large firms or those with complex business models. Instead of using manual spreadsheet–driven reconciliation and review processes, automation can be utilized to streamline process and reduce operational issues.

A WORD ON MARKET AND CREDIT RISKS

Two other important financial risks are market and credit. The responsibility for monitoring the firm's exposure to these risks will fall primarily to specialized departments; however, the compliance department plays an important role in monitoring and ensuring that controls around both risks are robust. These two financial risks are central to many large broker-dealers, as they will be engaged in businesses that have the potential to expose them to high degrees of market and credit risk.

Credit Risk

Credit risk is the potential for the firm to incur losses due to a customer's or counterparty's inability to meet its financial obligations. Generally, this risk will apply in some form to every broker-dealer. Large broker-dealers engage in customer financing as well as secured financing with other broker-dealers. Both of these activities carry credit risk because the broker-dealer is engaged in lending activity.

Credit risk is mitigated by strong controls and a governance framework that is designed to manage the risks. With respect to counterparty risk, the controls should provide for an onboarding process for new counterparties to determine their creditworthiness. Ultimately, this evaluation should result in the firm setting reasonable credit limits to prevent the customer from exposing the firm to dangerous amounts of credit risk. The firm's procedures should also call for periodic monitoring of counterparties for changes in creditworthiness and for other significant changes that could impact their credit rating.

The nature of the firm's risk limits and the process for dealing with breaches or manual overrides to the set limits are important concepts in credit risk. For example, if a firm has limits, but they may be exceeded without any automatic control preventing the breach, then the controls may not be adequate. Further, the firm's controls may not be adequate where the limits may be overridden by firm staff with no escalation or review by a supervisor or management.

Another important way firms mitigate credit risk is through a proper governance framework. This includes committees that have actual authority and insight into the firm's credit risk management. When working properly, the committees will include staff from various controls functions, including compliance. Committees should always act as an independent review and check on the businesses and need a sufficient degree of authority to accomplish this. Inadequately staffed committees or committees with no real power or role in important decisions are not going to be effective mitigants of credit risk.

Market Risk

Market risk is potential loss to the firm or customer due to an adverse movement in the price of a security or any other financial instrument. Generally, firms that do not have any proprietary inventory are not exposed to market risk in a material way. Conversely, all broker-dealers that hold securities for financial instruments for their own benefit are exposed to some degree of market risk. While most broker-dealers engage in hedging activity, perfect hedges are prohibitively costly. In short, a certain amount of market risk will always be left on the table even if the firm has taken action to reduce its market risk. As with credit risk, the broker-dealer should have controls and a governance framework designed to ensure it understands, monitors, and effectively mitigates its market risk.

The source of market risk for an individual firm can come from many places. Most firms are exposed to some degree of macroeconomic or systemic risk. These types of risks include geopolitical, currency, and interest rate risks. Systemic risk impacts the entire marketplace and has a broad-based impact. An example of a systemic event that had an impact on market risk was observed recently with the United Kingdom's referendum vote to leave the European Union. The vote's result in favor of "leave" was a surprise and caused volatility in capital markets across the globe, including in equities, interest rates, currencies, and commodities. "Brexit" is a prime example of how a geopolitical event can have a broad impact across many markets and market participants.

Another source of market risk is a more specific, idiosyncratic risk. This is the risk that a specific sector, company, or market will have an adverse impact on a broker-dealer. The concept of idiosyncratic market risk is fairly straightforward. For example, a firm may suffer severe losses if its entire inventory consists of the stock of one company and it comes out that there are accounting irregularities at that company. This same concept would apply to an entire sector or some other specific asset or asset class that is exposed to market risk.

Firms measure and mitigate market risk through the use of complicated models and statistical analysis. This sort of work is usually performed by specialists in the firm's market risk and risk management departments.

Like with credit risk, compliance still has a role to play in the management of market risk at a broker-dealer. A broker-dealer should have robust policies and procedures around the creation of risk limits, and a process for monitoring those limits and any exceptions that occur. For firms with large amounts of market risk, risk limits should be set at various levels. These could include firmwide, security-specific, sector-specific, individual trader, and desk limits. Overall, a broker-dealer must have a grasp on its market risk at any given time. It must also take steps to determine what its risk appetite is and have a system to prevent its risk from exceeding that level.

As with credit risk, committees and basic corporate governance have an important role to play in acting as an independent check on the business and control functions. The firm should have adequately staffed risk management and market risk committees that meet regularly and have sufficient authority to set and enforce risk limits.

CHAPTER 7

Cyber Risk Role in Governance Model and Compliance Framework

Alexander Abramov

Evolution of risk governance in capital markets was shaped by multiple forces, new products, new risks, new regulations (sometimes as a response to new risks). This chapter will discuss how emergence of Cyber Risk impacted risk governance models and how regulatory environment has changed to address this emergent risk.

CYBER RISK AS A PART OF OPERATIONAL RISK GOVERNANCE WITHIN THREE LINES OF DEFENSE MODEL

Q. What are your greatest concerns regarding financial stability . . . ?
A. In the current environment, my top five concerns about UK financial stability would be:
Operational/Cyber Risk: The focus on credit, market and liquidity risk over the past 5 years may have distracted attention from operational, and in particular Cyber Risks, among financial institutions and infrastructures. This is a rapidly rising area of risk with potentially systemic implications. It calls for a system-wide response.
Andrew Haldane, Bank of England's Chief Economist

The financial crisis of 2008 has provided many important lessons that go beyond the financial world. We've learned more about interplay of integration and systemic risk. Duncan Watts,[1] sociologist and principal researcher at Microsoft Research, demonstrated that deeper integration of a network does not have a direct impact on its stability. In fact, integration could be a double-edged sword—and the greater the degree of integration, the stronger the impact. As applied to financial systems, Andrew Haldane sees that "links in the system act as a mutual insurance device as risk is distributed and diversified away. That results in connected networks appearing 'robust' to shocks. But when shocks are sufficiently large, the same connectivity serves as a shock-transmitter. Risk-sharing becomes risk-spreading. Links in the system act as a mutual incendiary device as risk is amplified across the wider web. Connected networks become 'fragile.'"[2]

In a direct parallel to Cyber Risk, increased interconnectedness of information systems allows for better and faster threat identification and modeling; cooperation in cyber counterintelligence; and adversary hunt. It becomes a double-edge sword, though, as higher integration facilitates faster attack propagation and multiplies effects and damages across a larger number of financial institutions.

Technology Risk was part of the financial risk discipline as early as the days when mainframes began to be used in financial services in the 1960s. At the time, it was not recognized as a separate category of financial risk; however, it was an attendant component for other types of risk—whether it was with regard to the accuracy of NAV computation or trade netting and allocation.

Operational Risk had included originally just a few technology risk components, such as software or hardware risk to account for exposure across various risk categories. As the use of technology became more and more pervasive, additional Operational Risk controls became partially or completely technology dependent—reconciliations, confirmations, and reporting. As a matter of fact, it is hard to identify an Operational Risk control that is not technology dependent. Even employee training relies on content delivered by technology.

The fall of Barings Bank in 1995 was a significant wake-up call to the industry and a lesson in the importance of Operational Risk Management as well as Information Risk Management. There were multiple control breaks in this case, such as HR onboarding, lax audit practices, and inappropriate reporting structure, but by far the most drastic one was a lack of segregation of duties (SoD). Mr. Leeson, who single-handedly brought down the oldest established merchant bank (1762), had access as both a Baring's floor manager on SIMEX[3] and a Jakarta branch settlement clerk. He was able to balance his own books and settle his own trades. Regrettably, a lack of SoD continues to be one of the major factors in Information and Cyber Risk as we see it today.

In 2008, SocGen's Mr. Kerviel retained his back-office employee access after being promoted to equity index arbitrage trader. This deficiency in employee transfer process had a cost of over $7 billion to Société Générale. These types of deficiencies are also contributing to an increase of cyber risk.

In 2016, Bangladesh's central bank became a victim of hackers who had stolen $81 million from the bank's account at the Federal Reserve Bank of New York. According to Thomson Reuters,[4] the requests had been authenticated by SWIFT (Society for Worldwide Interbank Financial Telecommunication), the first line of defense against fraudulent wire transfers. The Federal Reserve Bank of New York did not find issues with most of the requests submitted by hackers; however, an attempt to transfer $20 million to a foundation in Sri Lanka was reversed because the word *foundation* was misspelled. According to the Thomson Reuters article, it had become clear that "deficiencies in training, lack of preventive controls and monitoring were the main contributors to this loss."[5]

The root causes of these three incidents are similar; the difference is that the first two were perpetrated by insiders and were not classified as cyber incidents at the time. The third one was caused by the outsiders (perhaps with insiders' complicity) and was clearly attributed to cybercrime. Over 20 years after the fall of Barings bank, financial institutions are still suffering losses caused by lack of robust user access control and SoD.

In 2014, the US intelligence leaders (CIA, FBI, and National Intelligence) stated[6] for the first time that the cyber attacks and the cyber espionage have supplanted terrorism as the top security threat facing the United States. According to James R. Clapper, Director of National Intelligence, "The world is applying digital technologies faster than our ability to understand the security implications and mitigate potential risks." In his 2016 Worldwide Threat Assessment of the US intelligence community,[7] Mr. Clapper spoke specifically about cyber threats to financial markets: "As we have already seen, false data and unanticipated algorithm behaviors have caused significant fluctuations in the stock market because of the reliance on automated trading of financial instruments."

The magnitude of potential cyber losses is staggering. According to Lloyd's and the report by the Centre for Risk Studies at the University of Cambridge, a major cyber attack on a US power grid could have a total impact to the US economy of $243 billion, rising to more than $1 trillion in the most extreme version of the scenario.[8]

To counteract these threats, the financial firms' Information Security Departments (ISDs) have missions to protect organization information assets. In a perfect world, they would stop all conceivable and inconceivable internal and external threats. In reality, the effectiveness of the ISDs' processes and tools is limited by legitimate business needs (required access to the information by trusted individuals) and growing sophistication of the adversaries. As the ISDs focus more on cybersecurity process and tools rather than on risk management, most financial firms have established Information Risk Management (IRM) groups to manage risks to information assets, including Cyber Risk.

IRM groups are charged with helping to establish the balance between the business needs and information asset protection based on firms' risk appetite. To accomplish its mission IRM creates governance, develops assessment methodologies, conducts risk assessments, and tracks issue completion. The US Department of Homeland Security recommends that Cyber Risk be incorporated "into existing risk management and governance processes."[9] Making Cyber Risk management a part of IRM and therefore part of Operational Risk would create a robust approach for managing, assessing, monitoring, and reporting enterprise risks.

From the early 2010s, financial firms have adopted Operational Risk governance that relies on the three lines of defense model. According to the IIA (Institute of Internal Auditors) position paper,

The Three Lines of Defense model distinguishes among three groups (or lines) involved in effective risk management:

- Functions that own and manage risks
- Functions that oversee risks
- Functions that provide independent assurance[10]

Cyber Risk plays a special role within each line of defense and has the following distinct characteristics, as outlined by the author:[11]

People:
- Elevated Conduct Risk
- Inadequate/ineffective business user training
- Communication barriers between Technology and Business (lack of common language/"translators")

Threats/Compliance/Risk Management:
- Quickly evolving threat landscape
- Active multiple adversaries
- Similar to Operational Risk, Cyber Risk events could not be predicted.
- Cyber Risk events and near misses may not be detected for days or longer
- Loss amount (intellectual property, personal identifiable information) may never be determined
- Diverse and increasing regulatory requirements that vary from country to country and state to state

- Cyber Risk insurance (risk transfer) market is immature; actuarial data are inadequate

Technology:

- Complexity of the firm's technical architecture, including reliance on third, fourth, ... *n*-parties' services
- Increased interconnectedness of the financial markets participants' systems
- Presence of legacy systems that are cumbersome to maintain in a secure state
- High amount of change in the firm's technical architecture
- Proliferation of adopted information and cybersecurity tools and lack of coordination of the tool output
- Shortage of skilled Information and Cyber Security staff

The first line of defense plays a major role in all aspects of Cyber Risk management. Many firms have in fact adopted an organizational design where Information and Cyber Risk teams are embedded in every line of business. These teams are led by *technology risk controllers* (TRCs) and consist of *technology risk liaisons* (TRLs) within Business and Technology areas. This matrix-type of organization has proven advantageous for the following reasons:

1. Ability to recruit or appoint people who are already involved in business processes or technology development:
   - Leveraging insider knowledge and existing relationships
   - Providing an opportunity for TRLs to learn a new craft and potentially provide an entry point to a new career in Cyber Risk
   - Facilitating promoting cyber awareness or secure coding practices within existing teams
2. Elasticity of the team size and flexibility in managing resources:
   - Utilizing wider bandwidth of the TRLs when required (managing cyber incidents; preparing and conducting cyber exercises; supporting risk assessments) and releasing resources when demand is low
   - Freeing the TRC from the need to manage a large team and relying instead on primary managers (TRC would still provide a performance evaluation and negotiate TRLs utilization with a primary manager)

There are certainly potential issues with this model that would include resource contention and challenges in recruiting TRLs with the correct basic skillset and training them. These issues would become manageable provided clear and formal governance and executive support are in place.

This organizational approach facilitates the definition of a bespoke Cyber Risk program that is tailored to a specific risk profile of the business unit and aligns with a firm's risk appetite. This approach also allows the close integration with other risk disciplines relevant to the business; provides effective coordination with other lines of defense as well as compliance, regulatory affairs, information and physical security teams; supports consistent interpretation and implementation of enterprise Cyber Risk policies; and facilitates effective and efficient execution of a Cyber Risk program.

The TRC function provides oversight of identity and access management. It is instrumental in making sure that the design of the access role does not contain SoD conflicts; that the roles granted within an application and for multiple applications do not create SoD issues; that the appropriate approver has authorized all access to be granted upon user onboarding and internal transfer; that access is reviewed periodically and unnecessary access is removed; and access is removed timely upon employment termination. FINRA Series 99 Operations Professional responsibilities include oversight of several activities we've just mentioned; it is therefore advisable for TRC to become FINRA Series 99 Registered Representative. Please refer to the section "Organizational Compliance and Supervision" in this chapter for more extensive treatment of this topic.

The first line of defense role is pivotal in influencing and shaping correct cyber behavior of every user in the organization.

There are several avenues counteracting social engineering, malware introduction, and raising cybersecurity awareness:

- Code-of-Conduct statement on appropriate employee cyber behavior with written acknowledgment
- Information security policies and procedures awareness and training
- Clear Desk Policy and compliance audits of it
- Cyber Risk poster campaigns
- U.S. National Cyber Security Month (October) events participation
- Information protection and Cyber Risk awareness annual training
- Anti-phishing training and exercises (Multiple studies have shown that conducting regular exercises decreases the rate of clicks on phishing e-mails. Also, those who did click a phishing link are up to 90% more likely to complete follow-up training.)

One of the most important success factors in shaping right behaviors is tone from the top and leading by example. As the EY study[12] has established, messages that are not cascaded effectively throughout the organization are a top cause of a breakdown in risk culture behavior.

Sometimes a very simple message from the top could have a profound effect. Several years ago, the author and his colleagues in the IT department received an e-mail from the CIO, titled "Clear Desk Policy." The e-mail contained two words—*my desk*—and a picture of CIO's desk featuring just his keyboard and a mouse, nothing else. In a few days the entire floor went through a significant transformation, as many colleagues wanted to emulate the CIO's minimalistic desk style.

Creating an engaging and effective Cyber Risk training program is a big and increasing challenge. In 1971, information theorist Herbert Simon wrote: "In an information-rich world, the wealth of information means a dearth of something else: A scarcity of whatever it is that information consumes. What information consumes is rather obvious: It consumes the attention of its recipients. Hence a wealth of information creates a poverty of attention."[13] To address rapidly diminishing attention spans (which, incidentally, affects all generations), Cyber Risk training instructional design increasingly includes a higher level of interaction, videos, and gamification.

The first line of defense also has an important role in the detection of insider cybercrimes. According to a Carnegie Mellon University study, most incidents were detected through an audit, customer complaint, or coworker suspicion:

- Routine or impromptu auditing was the most common way that an attack was detected (41%). In terms of who detected the attack, internal employees were the most common (54%), followed by customers (30%).
- Only 6% of the cases were known to involve the use of software and systems to detect the fraudulent activity.
- Transaction logs, database logs, and access logs were known to be used in the ensuing incident response for only 20% of the cases.[14]

An EY study has shown that at 94% of enterprises severe breaches to a firm's risk policies would result in disciplinary action.[15] Employee awareness that monitoring is in place and inappropriate behavior will lead to a disciplinary action may serve as a deterring control in some cases of insider threat.

The second line of defense includes Risk (IRM), Business Continuity Management (BCM), and Compliance. The IRM typically creates a firm's Cyber Risk governance framework and assesses its implementation. To borrow a well-known maxim from technology, deployment does not equal adoption—writing a policy does not mean people will be complying with it. To make a framework successful, it takes leadership, mastery of relationship management, and technical depth. This is where the TRCs and the first line of defense come into play, providing consistent and effective implementation of the firm's framework.

The IRM would conduct a Cyber Risk assessment as a part of technology project review or targeted Cyber Risk assessments. General-purpose application and infrastructure security assessments have significant focus on cybersecurity. Targeted assessments could cover specific aspects, such as network security, wireless security/site audit, or workstation/endpoint security.

Typically, these assessments would be application-centric (vs. data-centric) or specific to a certain layer (e.g., network) of the firm technology architecture. The information risk focus of business could be data-centric and sometimes could be application agnostic. The TRC role is to bridge that gap and to translate application assessment findings into issues relevant to business data, frame the issues in terms of business risk, and articulate them to the business leadership.

Compliance and regulators would conduct reviews and assessments based on country and legal entity applicable regulations. The role of the TRC in this process is to support business area respondents with advice and to help provide relevant evidence.

The third line of defense role is played by Audit departments. Cybersecurity is reviewed as part of SDLC (system development lifecycle) audits to ascertain that systems are developed with built-in security controls and that safe coding principles are used in the development process. Major system implementation audits would have cyber controls review included in the scope. A targeted cybersecurity audit would review implementation of the cybersecurity framework and program, the configuration and deployment of cybersecurity tools and systems, and employee cyber awareness programs.

The findings from audits and assessments conducted by the second and third lines of defense would be presented to the first line of defense and TRCs. TRCs would take a leadership role in amalgamating various stakeholders' requirements into a coherent and balanced Cyber Risks program consistent with the area risk appetite. TRC would then lead efficient execution of the program, providing expertise and professional program management and allowing business leaders more time to focus on simply running their business.

CYBER RISK INTEGRATION WITH OPERATIONAL RISK PROCESSES

[Risk Self-Assessment (RSA) is a] "tool to assess the processes underlying its operations against a library of potential threats and vulnerabilities and consider their potential impact. The Risk

Control Self-Assessment (RCSA) evaluates inherent risk (the risk before controls are considered), the effectiveness of the control environment, and residual risk (the risk exposure after controls are considered).[16]

> Basel Committee on Banking Supervision, BCBS 195,
> *"Principles for the Sound Management of Operational Risk,"*
> June 2011

Operational Risk uses a variety of tools and methods for risk measurement and reporting. RCSA and HLA (high-level assessment) are the core ones, supplemented by use of scenario analysis and business process mapping. Cyber Risk follows the taxonomy of Operational Risk terms and risk reporting requirements.

One of the key success factors for RCSA effectiveness is the appropriate definition of risk and control ownership. The Cyber Risk ownership is tightly linked with data; the data owners own the risk. Determining the data owners is not a trivial task in a large enterprise, and TRC helps to facilitate the search for appropriate owners and confirmation of the ownership. If the data ownership is unambiguously established, allocation of the loss would also be simplified.

The data ownership and attendant risk decisions could belong to a specific area of business; however, control ownership could be located in multiple areas, such as facilities, Information Security, BCM, or Operations. It is important that the control would be identified at the same level as risk (enterprise, process, activity), and every control should be linked to a control objective.

The RCSA for a business unit is conducted via discussions with business leadership and collecting data from several sources, including Operations and, for Cyber Risk items, Information Security. The TRC would play a major role in helping to provide an aggregate view of risks and controls as related to cybersecurity, vendor information risk, and end-user computing. BCM plays a similar role in providing a view on business continuity risks and controls.

As Operational Risk requires *loss data collection and analysis*, Cyber Risk contributes the data related to losses from cyber incidents. Generally, the size of a loss should not be the only trigger for reporting, as sometimes small losses from several business units could aggregate to a material loss for the enterprise. For Cyber Risk, it is especially relevant, as a small loss or a near-miss could mask a significant latent issue that could go undiscovered for a long time.

If a cyber-loss event requires a root-cause analysis, this process would involve the firm's Computer Security Incident Response Team (CSIRT), and, when warranted, country regulators and law enforcement agencies (FBI, Scotland Yard). If the firm does not have an established CSIRT, then a multidisciplinary group could be convened to conduct an investigation and analysis. The group could include Information Security, HR, Technology, Security, Legal, Compliance, Communications, Operations, and other stakeholders.

Operational Risk reporting includes definition and tracking of key risk indicators (KRIs)—metrics designed to measure inherent risk—and key performance indicators (KPIs)—designed to measure the adequacy of underlying processes and controls.

The definition of meaningful and clear metrics (or KRIs and KPIs) is essential for managing risk effectively and requires many iterations. The definitions and thresholds also need to be reviewed periodically (usually quarterly) and to be adjusted based on business environment and risk appetite.

It is recommended to have a small number of meaningful indicators, rather than to try covering the complexity of the business with many narrow or specific indicators. For Cyber Risk indicators, it would be important to cover all relevant domains where controls are present to drive accountability to these areas. Some of the key areas for Cyber Risk KPIs could be:

- Vulnerability Management (VM)—owned by Information Security (e.g., number of high-risk vulnerabilities not remediated within a certain period of time)
- Data Loss Prevention (DLP)—owned by Information Security (e.g., number of data exfiltration attempts)
- User-access reviews—owned by Business (e.g., number of past-due user-access reviews)
- Cyber-awareness—owned by Business (e.g., number of clicks on anti-phishing e-mails)
- Secure coding—owned by Technology (e.g., number of vulnerabilities detected per number of lines of code)

According to a study by the Ponemon Institute, while 75% of the US respondents said metrics were either "important" or "very important," more than half either said that their firms' existing metrics were not aligned with business objectives, or the respondent was unsure whether they were aligned.[17]

Operational Risk also uses scenario analysis as a process to obtain the expert opinions of business line and risk managers and to identify potential Operational Risk events and assess their potential outcome.[18] Scenario analysis is helpful in supplementing the RCSA and other Operational Risk management tools by focusing on low-probability but high-impact events that the other tools may have missed.

CYBER RISK MEASUREMENT AND ASSESSMENT FRAMEWORKS

Measure what is measurable, and make measurable what is not so.
Galileo Galilei

ISACA IT Governance Institute, in its "Information Security Governance: Guidance for Boards of Directors and Executive Management," defined five outcomes of governance related to organization-wide risk management:[19]

- Strategic alignment of risk management decisions with missions and business functions consistent with organizational goals and objectives
- Execution of risk management processes to frame, assess, respond to, and monitor risk to organizational operations and assets, individuals, other organizations, and the nation
- Effective and efficient allocation of risk management resources
- Performance-based outcomes by measuring, monitoring, and reporting risk management metrics to ensure that organizational goals and objectives are achieved
- Delivered value by optimizing risk management investments in support of organizational objectives

The need for risk governance and measurement has wide consensus; however, approaches to how to measure risk are many. We will review approaches based on the National Institute of Standards and Technology (NIST); ISO (the International Organization for Standardization); ISACA, and several other frameworks.

NIST is a non-regulatory agency of the U.S. Department of Commerce. The Computer Security Resource Center (CSRC) is part of one of the six NIST laboratory units called Information Technology Laboratory (ITL). CSRC publishes NIST Special Publications (SPs); SP 800 subseries (computer security) cover security and privacy guidelines, recommendations, and assessment frameworks. SP 800 subseries are developed by the Joint Task Force Transformation Initiative Interagency Working Group with representatives from the Civil, Defense, and Intelligence communities. A large credit for developing these publications goes to Dr. Ron Ross, JTF leader, who is also the principal architect of the Risk Management Framework.

In February 2014, NIST published the Framework for Improving Critical Infrastructure Cybersecurity Version 1.0.[20] Even as the document is focusing on critical infrastructure, its applicability (and adoption) goes far beyond, as its principles are relevant to any enterprise. The Framework is a risk-based approach to managing cybersecurity risk and is composed of three parts: the Framework Core, the Framework Implementation Tiers, and the Framework Profiles.

The Framework Core describes cybersecurity activities, desired outcomes, and cross-references a number of other frameworks. The Framework Core consists of five concurrent and, importantly, continuous functions—Identify, Protect, Detect, Respond, and Recover.

The Framework Implementation Tiers help to measure organization maturity in its implementation of the Cyber Risk program from Partial (Tier 1) to Risk Informed (Tier 2), to Repeatable (Tier 3), to Adaptive (Tier 4).

A Framework Profile helps to develop organizations' current risk profile and a target risk profile that could be used to support prioritization and measurement of progress toward the target profile.

Similarly to NIST, ISO publishes standards focusing on risk governance and technology controls assessment.

ISACA,[21] the global membership association for IT and information systems professionals, publishes COBIT (Control Objectives for Information and Related Technology). COBIT 5 is a business and management framework for governance and management of enterprise IT. It is based on five broad principles and includes seven supporting enablers, contained within Principle 4: Enabling a Holistic Approach. The enablers are factors that, individually and collectively, influence whether something would work—in this case, governance and management over enterprise IT. These seven enablers are:

1. Principles, policies, and frameworks—the vehicles to translate the desired behavior into practical guidance for day-to-day management.
2. Processes—an organized set of practices and activities to achieve certain objectives and produce a set of outputs in support of achieving overall IT-related goals.
3. Organizational structures.
4. Culture, ethics, and behavior of individuals.
5. Information—required for keeping the organization running and well governed; but at the operational level, information is often the key product of the enterprise itself.
6. Services, infrastructure, and applications—include the infrastructure, technology, and applications that provide the enterprise with information technology processing and services.
7. People, skills, and competencies.

NIST, ISO, and ISACA Risk Assessment Governance and Guidance

NIST 800-30, "Guide for Conducting Risk Assessments," is one of the most authoritative and referenced publications on Cyber Risk. It creates taxonomy and definitions for key Cyber Risk concepts and shows how to conduct risk assessments, step by step.[22]

NIST 800-39, "Managing Information Security Risk Organization, Mission, and Information System View," sets forth definitions for Information Risk management and describes processes along three tiers: Organization, mission/business process, and information system. The document makes an appropriate disclaimer:

> Managing information security risk, like risk management in general, is not an exact science. It brings together the best collective judgments of individuals and groups within organizations responsible for strategic planning, oversight, management, and day-to-day operations—providing both the necessary and sufficient risk response measures to adequately protect the missions and business functions of those organizations.[23]

ISO Standard 31010, 2009 "Risk Management—Risk Assessment Techniques," provides guidance on selection and application of systematic techniques for risk assessment. There are 31 techniques described in the standard, including scenario analysis, root-cause analysis (RCA), fault tree analysis (FTA), failure mode and effects analysis (FMEA), Monte Carlo simulation, Bayesian statistics, and Bayesian nets.

The standard frames risk assessment around these fundamental questions:

- What can happen and why (by risk identification)?
- What are the consequences?
- What is the probability of their future occurrence?
- Are there any factors that mitigate the consequence of the risk or that reduce the probability of the risk?
- Is the level of risk tolerable or acceptable and does it require further treatment?[24]

ISACA has published COBIT 5 for Risk to provide guidance on how to use the COBIT 5 framework to establish the risk governance and management functions for the enterprise and how to create a structured approach to use the COBIT 5 principles to govern and manage IT risk.

COBIT 5 for Risk presents two perspectives on how to use COBIT 5 in a risk context: Risk function and risk management. The risk function perspective focuses on what is needed to build and sustain the risk function within an enterprise. The risk management perspective focuses on the core risk governance and management processes of how to optimize risk and how to identify, analyze, respond to, and report on risk on a daily basis.[25]

COBIT 5 contains a set of enablers, and COBIT 5 for Risk provides guidance and describes how each enabler contributes to the overall governance and management of the risk function. For example:

- Which *processes* are required to define and sustain the risk function, govern and manage risk?
- What *information flows* are required to govern and manage risk—for example, risk universe, risk profile?
- What *organizational structures* are required to govern and manage risk effectively—for example, enterprise risk committee, risk function?
- What *people and skills* should be put in place to establish and operate an effective risk function?[26]

It is important to note that COBIT 5 for Risk addresses all ISO 31000 principles through the COBIT 5 for Risk principles and enablers models.

NIST, ISO, and FAIR Risk Assessment Frameworks

NIST Special Publications 800-53, "Security and Privacy Controls for Federal Information Systems and Organizations," and 800-53a, "Assessing Security and Privacy Controls in Federal Information Systems and Organizations Building Effective Assessment Plans," are two large volumes of almost 500 pages each that provide comprehensive guidance on security and privacy control selection (determining what controls are needed to manage risks to organizational operations and assets) and the security assessment and privacy assessment processes. These publications show how to build effective assessment plans and how to analyze and manage assessment results.

NIST 800-53A underlines a very important principle:

Security control assessments and privacy control assessments are not about checklists, simple pass-fail results, or generating paperwork to pass inspections or audits—rather, such assessments are the principal vehicle used to verify that implemented security controls and privacy controls are meeting their stated goals and objectives.[27]

Unfortunately, in some organizations completing checklists is the end game of the risk and control assessments. The same publication cautions that "the assessment process is an information-gathering activity, not a security- or privacy-producing activity."[28] Adopting one of the frameworks and implementing it in-depth throughout the organization would allow gaining real value from the process and aligning it with strategic goals of the enterprise.

ISO standard ISO/IEC 27002:2013, "Information Technology—Security Techniques—Code of Practice for Information Security Controls,"[29] defines three main sources of security requirements:

1. The assessment of risks to the organization, taking into account the organization's overall business strategy and objectives. Through a risk assessment, threats to assets are identified, vulnerability to and likelihood of occurrence is evaluated, and potential impact is estimated.
2. The legal, statutory, regulatory, and contractual requirements that an organization, its trading partners, contractors, and service providers have to satisfy, and their sociocultural environment.
3. The set of principles, objectives, and business requirements for information handling, processing, storing, communicating, and archiving that an organization has developed to support its operations.

The standard defines the controls framework across multiple domains, including governance, asset management, access control, cryptography, operations security, BCM, system acquisition, development, and maintenance.

Jack Jones and Jack Freund have developed an innovative approach measuring and managing Information Risk.[30] Factor Analysis of Information Risk (FAIR), in their words, "provides a proven and credible framework for understanding, measuring, and analyzing Information Risk of any size or complexity." The methodology includes risk theory, risk calculation, scenario modeling, and communicating risk within the organization. The strongest suits of FAIR are fine-tuned terms that form an ontology (vs. taxonomy) with well-defined relationships and rigorous logical approach in conducting risk assessments. The approach is based on leveraging sometimes unconscious ways that humans estimate values to come up with inputs to the model. The framework founders call this approach deductive (à la Sherlock Holmes), where we infer model elements based on our experience, logic, and critical thinking. Therefore, deductive modeling (as opposed to inductive) is less sensitive to data quality, but depends on level of experience and analytical capabilities of the model builders.

Another strong side of FAIR is definition of controls and control categories. FAIR distinguishes among asset-level, variance, and decision-making controls.

Asset-level controls apply to the asset directly, like a lock on a safe, whereas variance controls are governance based (policies, guidance, and training). Decision-making controls help to detect or prevent what could be unsound or faulty decisions. These controls would include metrics, reporting, and surveillance. Analyzing controls using this mindset could be helpful, as it could lead to better balance in overall control framework. For example, which is better, having weaker policies with less variance or stronger policies with more variance? The author votes for the former choice.

Another interesting risk assessment approach was proposed by Peter Sandman,[31] who has postulated, "Risk = Hazard + Outrage." His approach, as applied to Cyber Risk, adds a measure of reputational risk into an otherwise technical discussion of how many desktops could be compromised and what amount of fines would be levied by the regulator or courts. In a situation of low hazard/high outrage, certain adjustments could be made to issue prioritization and mitigation.

CYBER RISK REGULATION OVERVIEW

Cybersecurity risk, as with all risks, cannot be completely eliminated, but instead must be managed through informed decision-making processes.

U.S. Department of Energy[32]

Regulators recognized the importance of many controls that serve as the bedrock of Cyber Risk management even before Cyber Risk was recognized as a discipline. Principles of appropriate access, SoD, and client asset protection were embedded in regulations for decades. A number of regulations for public companies and national banks (that covered many broker-dealers) had mandated Cyber Risk controls implementation; the most notable example is the Sarbanes–Oxley Act of 2002, Section 404: Assessment of Internal Control Requirement to Evaluate Controls Designed to Prevent or Detect Fraud.

Since the mid-2000s regulators and SROs have been increasingly active in the cyber arena. Cybersecurity has been a regular theme in the FINRA Regulatory and Examination Priorities Letter since 2007. In 2010 and 2011, it conducted on-site reviews to understand how firms control critical information technology and cyber risks. In 2014, FINRA launched a targeted examination (sweep) to explore cybersecurity.

FINRA had four primary objectives:

1. To better understand the types of threats that firms face
2. To increase understanding of firms' risk appetite, exposure, and major areas of vulnerabilities in their information technology systems

3. To better understand firms' approaches to managing these threats
4. To share observations and findings with firms

FINRA published the Report on Cybersecurity Practices[33] in February 2015, detailing findings and best practices identified. Not surprisingly, FINRA cited major frameworks that are widely adopted by the industry; some of them were reviewed earlier in this chapter:

- NIST Framework for Improving Critical Infrastructure Cybersecurity Version 1.0
- NIST Special Publication 800-53
- ISO/IEC Information Technology 27001 and 27002 framework
- ISACA 7 Control Objectives for Information and Related Technology (COBIT) 5
- Payment Card Industry (PCI) Data Security Standard (DSS)

FINRA reports that nearly 90% of firms used one or more of the NIST, ISO, or ISACA frameworks or standards. A number of firms noted that the frameworks and standards could improve communication, both within the firm and with the third parties. Their use could help establish a common vocabulary that enhances understanding and precision in communications. Developing this common vocabulary is an iterative learning process that takes time, but which can pay dividends down the road. For example, it can reduce the likelihood of misalignment between risk appetite and controls. Several firms noted that it had improved their ability to communicate with the board on cybersecurity issues. That in turn led to enhanced support, including funding, for cybersecurity initiatives.[34]

In addition to review of framework use, FINRA has also conducted review of metrics, defense-in-depth approaches; I&AM (Identity and Access Management), incident response planning; vendor management; staff training; cyber intelligence and information sharing; and cyber insurance.

An interesting aspect of the FINRA report is identification of linkages between several predicate rulings and the cybersecurity realm:

- Asset inventory process—identifying critical assets is firms' obligation under Rule 30 of SEC Regulation S-P to protect customers' personally identifiable information (PII).
- Incident response plan—notification obligations pursuant to SEC Regulation S-ID (Red Flags Rule) state reporting requirements and FINRA rules. Specifically, the incident response plan should identify the parties to be notified, what information should be reported, when the parties are to be notified, and what information should be reported and when. Appropriate plan should aid the firm to provide notifications in a full, accurate, and timely fashion.

- In addition to FINRA Rule 4530(b) requirements, firms are encouraged to report material cyber incidents that do not trigger a reporting obligation to their regulatory coordinator.
- Cyber awareness—not specifically linked to a regulation; however, FINRA states that as cybersecurity threats may originate from clients, then many broker-dealers would provide cybersecurity education, especially if a customer's account has been attacked. Examples of potential customer-specific resources include recommendations for creating secure passwords and how to detect indications of social engineering attacks. FINRA believes this type of customer education can be beneficial, particularly since it can help reduce the likelihood that the same customers will be victimized again.

NFA has published Compliance Rules 2-9, 2-36, and 2-49, information systems security programs that became effective in March 2016. Similarly to FINRA, NFA references ISACA COBIT, the NIST Cybersecurity Framework, as well as best practices and standards promulgated by the SANS Institute (SANS), and the Open Web Application Security Project (OWASP).

Broker-dealers that are subsidiaries of banks under Federal Reserve supervision were required to participate in stress testing as mandated by Section 165(i) of the Dodd-Frank Wall Street Reform and Consumer Protection Act. National banks and federal savings associations with total consolidated assets over $10 billion are to conduct annual stress tests as prescribed by the OCC in 12 CFR 46.

As the major banks have been the main focus of stress testing, broker-dealers have faced a lower level of scrutiny, since they were not seen as posing the same level of systemic threat. However, increasingly, the regulators have been looking at ways to safeguard the broker-dealer sector, which accounts for $4.7 trillion in total assets, according to the Federal Reserve.

Thomson Reuters[35] reports that the broker-dealers under review by FINRA in 2015 included those in the $50-billion-and-below asset range for the first time, bringing heightened regulatory oversight to brokers previously not considered as posing systemic risk, compared with the $1-trillion-plus asset banks considered too big to fail.

"If firms do not contemplate a sufficiently severe stress environment, they may face problems during the next crisis," said Bill Wollman, executive vice president FINRA Member Regulation, Risk Oversight, and Operational Regulation, who cited the Lehman and MF Global failures as evidence that even the savviest Wall Street brokers pose threats if safeguards are not in place.

As part of a stress test, banks are required to prepare and file the Dodd-Frank Act Stress Test (DFAST) schedules and ensure that they reflect a fair presentation of the banks' financial condition and assessment of performance under stressed scenarios. The required scenarios would include DFAST Baseline Scenario, DFAST Adverse Scenario, and DFAST Severely Adverse Scenario.

An idiosyncratic workshop that would help to estimate operational losses under the CCAR Testing Exercise could include Cyber Risk–related scenarios, such as:

- Intentional corruption of algorithmic trading code
- DDoS attack on trading platform

Working on these scenario analyses would not be a completely new task for capital markets' Operational Risk, Cyber Risk, and Trading and Technology participants.

The firms conduct their internal cyber exercises with scenarios tailored for the enterprise, and sometimes for specific business units. The TRC as an organizer and lead facilitator would ensure the right level of representation and attendance at the exercise. As scenarios are being presented and discussed, observations and takeaways are being recorded. A post-exercise report would summarize the takeaways and convert some of them into actionable items.

For a number of years, several industry associations like the Securities Industry and Financial Markets Association (SIFMA) have conducted joint cyber exercises to check readiness and coordination between capital markets participants. The value of the streetwide exercises is in getting the participants to work together and interact, and also to obtain takeaways that could be used in internal exercises.

In November 2011, the Financial Services Sector Coordinating Council (FSSCC) hosted the first US marketwide cyber-disruption exercise called Quantum Dawn. The event has exercised risk practices across equities clearing and trading processes in response to infrastructure disruption, allowing firms to exercise their internal incident response plans in conjunction with each other, the FSSCC, and the FBI.

The SIFMA held the Quantum Dawn 2 exercise in July 2013. The exercise utilized a tool (called DECIDE) that was developed by Cyber Strategies, a division of NUARI (Norwich University Applied Research Institute). Over 500 individuals from approximately 50 entities participated, including financial firms, exchanges, and US government agencies. The following seven scenarios were used:[36]

1. Creation of an automatic sell-off in target stocks by using stolen administrator accounts

2. Introduction of counterfeit and malicious telecommunication equipment to divert attention and slow the investigation into the automatic selloff
3. Substantiation of the price drop by issuing fraudulent press releases on target stocks
4. Disruption of governmental websites and services through a distributed denial-of-service (DDoS) attack
5. Corruption of the source code of a financial application widely used in the equities market
6. Degradation of the credibility of an industry group by sending a phishing e-mail to harvest user names and passwords and submitting false information on the attack
7. Disruption of technology service by unleashing a custom virus with the goal of degrading post-trade processing

The SIFMA held the Quantum Dawn 3 exercise in September 2015. Over 650 participants from over 80 financial institutions and government agencies were part of the exercise, including the US Department of the Treasury, the Department of Homeland Security, the Federal Bureau of Investigation, federal regulators, and the Financial Services Information Sharing and Analysis Center (FS-ISAC). QD3 cyberattack scenarios included:

1. Domain Name System (DNS) Attack
2. Distributed Denial of Service (DDoS) Attack
3. Insider PII Breach Loss of Availability Settlement System
4. Compromise (Malware)[37]

Not all scenarios presented were relevant to every firm. In 2015 only some of the scenarios were presented to each firm.

The relevance of the scenarios is extremely important. For instance, a stock exchange or an institutional trading area may not have a significant risk associated with a loss of PII. That scenario would be a lot more relevant to a retail brokerage business. Internet-facing properties for a stock exchange or an institutional trading area would have an air gap to their main processing systems. For instance, a DDoS attack may not be a significant risk factor for these entities. Conversely, the following three scenarios from Quantum Dawn 2 (2013) would be valuable to use at the exercise for an exchange or an institutional trading area:

1. Introduction of counterfeit and malicious telecommunication equipment to divert attention and slow the investigation into the automatic sell-off
2. Corruption of the source code of a financial application widely used in the equities market

3. Disruption of technology service by unleashing a custom virus with the goal of degrading post-trade processing

Quantum Dawn IV took place in November 2017 and was again coordinated by SIFMA, utilizing NUARI DECIDE FS software. Over 900 participants from over 50 financial institutions and government agencies participated in the exercise.

The author was a part of a small advisory group that helped to shape the exercise tool in the late 2000s. Since then, the tool, as well as the methodology of the exercise, has evolved significantly. The exercises in 2015 and 2017 had deemphasized the use of the tool, as some complexity was removed in favor of more real-time interactions.

The role of government agencies and regulators in the exercise has evolved as well. From mere observers in the first iteration of the exercise, they became participants in the 2015 and 2017 exercises. The firms were expected to contact the agencies or law enforcement directly, if the exercise situation would warrant, to report and consult.

According to SIFMA,

The Quantum Dawn exercises are one component of SIFMA's comprehensive work with our members on a variety of cybersecurity initiatives. The financial industry is committed to furthering the development of industry-wide cybersecurity initiatives that protect our clients and critical business infrastructure, improve data sharing between public and private entities and safeguard customer information.[38]

Outside of the United States, the Cyber Security Agency of Singapore (CSA), in partnership with the Monetary Authority of Singapore (MAS), held its first cybersecurity tabletop exercise, CyberArk IV, for the banking and finance sector in May 2015. Over 60 participants took part in the exercise.

The New York State Department of Financial Services (DFS) supervises many different types of institutions, including banks and trust companies, credit unions, investment companies, savings banks, and savings and loan associations. Although it does not supervise broker-dealers, NYS DFS's "Cybersecurity Requirements for Financial Services Companies" (23 NYCRR Part 500) regulation, which took effect on March 1, 2017, is instructive to review in the context of this chapter. This regulation is groundbreaking in several respects, in particular that it includes very specific requirements in many categories. Among the major elements in the regulation are detailed requirements for

- Cybersecurity, third-party service provider security policies, and incident response plan.
- Appointing a chief information security officer.

- Deployment of key technologies, including encryption, multifactor authentication.
- Conducting annual penetration testing and biannual vulnerability assessments, "including any systematic scans or reviews of Information Systems reasonably designed to identify publicly known cybersecurity vulnerabilities."[39]
- Reporting to DFS within 72 hours any cybersecurity event "having a reasonable likelihood of materially harming any material part of the normal operation(s) of the Covered Entity."[40]
- Providing an annual written statement certifying that the entity is in compliance with the requirements set forth in this regulation.

The notable part of the regulation is that it requires implementing of controls, including encryption, to protect nonpublic information held or transmitted by the firm both in transit over external networks and at rest. The nonpublic information category is exceedingly broad and includes certain internal information that is not considered to be confidential. The regulation does allow, though, in lieu of encryption, using effective alternative compensating controls reviewed and approved by the firm's CISO.

NYS DFS's "Cybersecurity Requirements for Financial Services Companies" regulation provides insight as to where potentially other regulators may be looking to strengthen current cybersecurity requirements for financial firms.

ORGANIZATIONAL COMPLIANCE AND SUPERVISION

On June 16, 2011, the SEC approved FINRA Rule 1230(b)(6), which established a registration category and qualification examination requirement for operations professionals. To obtain the registration and become registered representatives (RRs), individuals require passing the Series 99 examination and being associated with a member firm.

The examination covers the following areas:

- Basic knowledge associated with the securities industry
- Basic knowledge associated with broker-dealer operations
- Professional conduct and ethical considerations

Upon passing the test, the results are posted to the FINRA Central Registration Depository (CRD).

Additionally, under FINRA Rule 1250 (Continuing Education Requirements), every person registered as an operations professional is subject to Regulatory Element and Firm Element continuing education.

Out of 16 categories of activities for this registration we will focus on the following three that are relevant to Cyber Risk discipline:[41]

1. Defining and approving business requirements for sales and trading systems and any other systems related to the covered functions, and validation that these systems meet such business requirements
2. Defining and approving business security requirements and policies for information technology, including, but not limited to, systems and data, in connection with the covered functions
3. Defining and approving information entitlement policies in connection with the covered functions

The first item deals with information system requirements that would include processing functionality, user interface, reporting, as well as information security and data protection model. The RR responsibilities could include:

- Ensuring appropriate classification of data processed by the system.
- Reviewing data validation approaches and data integrity checks, including interface controls.
- Verifying application of required data protection controls (e.g., encryption).
- Approving security model and SoD requirements. This includes review of toxic combinations (incompatible roles) within the system as well as between multiple systems.
- Verifying that appropriate resiliency controls are in place (e.g., protection from DDoS attacks).
- Verifying that testing methodology and design are adequate, cover and are traceable to all functional security requirements.
- Conducting periodic assessments to ascertain continuing compliance with current requirements.

The second item covers responsibilities related to Cyber Risk and information governance and could include creating broker-dealer-specific policies, standards, and procedures:

- Information Security Policy
- Data Classification Policy
- Identity and Access Management Standard
- End-User Computing Policy and Procedure
- Data Encryption Standard
- Data Erasure and Media Destruction Standard

- Authentication and Authorization Standard
- Application Security Standard
- Network Security Standard
- Cloud Security Standard
- System-Hardening Standards
- Cyber-Exercise Guidelines

The third item expands upon application roles design and covers specific sets of entitlements that would constitute a role in the system. Attention needs to be paid that a role would not have incompatible entitlements. Examples of the incompatible entitlements are:

- Client onboarding and wire release
- SSI (Standard Settlement Instruction) setup and trade
- Limit change and exception approval

Some entitlements should not be combined with any other entitlements, except read-only role, for example:

- User administration
- Technology roles (e.g., configuration changes)

Some firms have chosen to implement *role-based access control* (RBAC). Under this arrangement, certain roles (e.g., reconciliation clerk, trader assistant, account setup) would have a listed schedule of system entitlements across all systems of the entire enterprise. If someone is hired or transferred to take one of the defined roles, then user administration would grant that role to the individual and revoke all other assigned roles. The benefits of this approach are obvious:

- Granting and revoking access takes a minimal amount of time
- All employees assigned to the role have uniform access
- Rate of errors in granting access is greatly reduced

The drawbacks of the approach are:

- As the systems change, every role needs to be maintained. With a large number of roles, it becomes an arbitrage between increasing staff to maintain the roles and granting/revoking access.
- For small teams, it may not be feasible to create roles as every member may have a unique role.

- If the system has many regional, branch, and other variable entitlements, number of roles will become very large and difficult to manage and maintain. To reduce number of roles, a hybrid system could be used where a majority of entitlements would be grouped into the roles and some would be granted outside of the roles.

The firms need to assess with the help of their Series 99 RR what is the best model of access control administration that would fit the firm's risk appetite, system complexity, and operational capabilities.

In conclusion, Cyber Risk is still an emerging discipline, continuing to be shaped by new threats, new technology, with attendant new vulnerabilities, but also by new types of controls and new regulations, new defense strategies and tools, and the creativity of Cyber, Information, and Technology Risk professionals committed to the firm's and clients' information assets protection.

NOTES

1. Duncan Watts, "A Simple Model of Global Cascades on Random Networks," *Proceedings of the National Academy of Sciences of the United States of America*, Vol. 99, No. 9 (2002), http://www.pnas.org/content/99/9/5766.full
2. A. Haldane, "Why Institutions Matter (More Than Ever)," Centre for Research on Socio-Cultural Change (CRESC) Annual Conference, School of Oriental and African Studies, London (September 4, 2013), http://www.bankofengland.co .uk/publications/Documents/speeches/2013/speech676.pdf
3. The Singapore International Monetary Exchange (SIMEX) merged with the Stock Exchange of Singapore (SES) and the Securities Clearing and Computer Services Pte Ltd. (SCCS) in 1999 to form the Singapore Exchange (SGX).
4. Thomson Reuters, "Exclusive: NY Fed First Rejected Cyber-Heist Transfers, Then Moved $81 Million" (June 3, 2016), http://www.reuters.com/article/ us-cyber-heist-bangladesh-exclusive-idUSKCN0YQ041
5. Ibid.
6. Thomson Reuters, "Cyber Attacks Leading Threat against U.S.: Spy Agencies" (March 12, 2013), http://www.reuters.com/article/us-usa-threats -idUSBRE92B0LS20130312
7. J. Clapper, "Worldwide Threat Assessment of the U.S. Intelligence Community," (February 9, 2016), https://www.dni.gov/files/documents/SASC_Unclassified_ 2016_ATA_SFR_FINAL.pdf
8. Lloyd's, "New Lloyd's Study Highlights Wide Ranging Implications of Cyber Attacks" (July 8, 2015), http://www.lloyds.com/news-and-insight/press-centre/ press-releases/2015/07/business-blackout

9. Cyber Risk Management Primer for CEOs, U.S. DHS (January 21, 2018) https://www.dhs.gov/sites/default/files/publications/C3%20Voluntary%20Program%20-%20Cyber%20Risk%20Management%20Primer%20for%20CEOs%20_5.pdf

10. IAA, "The Three Lines of Defense in Effective Risk Management and Control" (January 2013), https://na.theiia.org/standards-guidance/Public%20Documents/PP%20The%20Three%20Lines%20of%20Defense%20in%20Effective%20Risk%20Management%20and%20Control.pdf

11. Alexander Abramov et al., "Cyber Risk, Risk Books" (September 2016), http://riskbooks.com/cyber-risk

12. EY, "2015 Risk Management Survey of Major Financial Institutions—Rethinking Risk Management: Banks Focus on Nonfinancial Risks and Accountability," p. 17.

13. H. A. Simon, "Designing Organizations for an Information-Rich World," in Martin Greenberger, *Computers, Communication, and the Public Interest* (John Hopkins Press, 1971), pp. 38–52.

14. CERT® Insider Threat Center at Carnegie Mellon University's Software Engineering Institute, "Insider Threat Study: Illicit Cyber Activity Involving Fraud in the U.S. Financial Services Sector" (July 2012), p. 9, http://resources.sei.cmu.edu/asset_files/SpecialReport/2012_003_001_28137.pdf

15. EY, "2015 Risk Management Survey of Major Financial Institutions—Rethinking Risk Management: Banks Focus on Nonfinancial Risks and Accountability," p. 17.

16. Basel Committee on Banking Supervision, BCBS 195, "Principles for the Sound Management of Operational Risk" (June 2011), p. 12, http://www.bis.org/publ/bcbs195.pdf

17. Ponemon Institute, "The State of Risk-Based Security: US & UK," 2013 Research Report, pp. 15–18, http://www.tripwire.com/ponemon/2013/

18. Basel Committee on Banking Supervision, BCBS 195, "Principles for the Sound Management of Operational Risk" (June 2011), p. 12.

19. ISACA IT Governance Institute, "Information Security Governance: Guidance for Boards of Directors and Executive Management" (2006), p. 13, http://www.isaca.org/Knowledge-Center/Research/Documents/Information-Security-Govenance-for-Board-of-Directors-and-Executive-Management_res_Eng_0510.pdf

20. NIST, "Framework for Improving Critical Infrastructure Cybersecurity Version 1.0" (February 12, 2014), https://www.nist.gov/sites/default/files/documents/cyberframework/cybersecurity-framework-021214.pdf

21. ISACA, http://www.isaca.org/cobit/pages/default.aspx

22. NIST Special Publication 800-30, "Guide for Conducting Risk Assessments" (September 2012), http://nvlpubs.nist.gov/nistpubs/Legacy/SP/nistspecialpublication800-30r1.pdf

23. NIST Special Publication 800-39, "Managing Information Security Risk Organization, Mission, and Information System View" (March 2011), http://nvlpubs.nist.gov/nistpubs/Legacy/SP/nistspecialpublication800-39.pdf

24. ISO/IEC 31010:2009, "Risk Management—Risk Assessment Techniques" (2009), https://www.iso.org/obp/ui/#iso:std:iec:31010:ed-1:v1:en

25. ISACA, COBIT 5 for Risk (2013), https://www.isaca.org/COBIT/Documents/COBIT-5-for-Risk-Preview_res_eng_0913.pdf

26. ISACA, COBIT 5 for Risk (2013), https://www.isaca.org/COBIT/Pages/Risk-product-page.aspx

27. NIST Special Publication 800-53A, Revision 4 "Assessing Security and Privacy Controls in Federal Information Systems and Organizations Building Effective Assessment Plans" (December 2014), p. xi, http://nvlpubs.nist.gov/nistpubs/SpecialPublications/NIST.SP.800-53Ar4.pdf

28. Ibid., p. 3.

29. ISO/IEC 27002:2013, Information Technology—Security Techniques—Code of Practice for Information Security Controls (2013), https://www.iso.org/obp/ui/#iso:std:iso-iec:27002:ed-2:v1:en

30. J. Freund and J. Jones, *Measuring and Managing Information Risk* (Oxford, UK: Elsevier, 2015).

31. P. Sandman, Biography (June 18, 2014), http://www.psandman.com/bio.htm

32. U.S. Department of Energy (DOE), Risk Management Process (May 23, 2012), https://energy.gov/oe/services/cybersecurity/cybersecurity-risk-management-process-rmp

33. FINRA, "Report on Cybersecurity Practices" (February 2015), http://www.finra.org/sites/default/files/p602363%20Report%20on%20Cybersecurity%20Practices_0.pdf

34. Ibid., p. 10.

35. Thomson Reuters, "Broker-Dealers Face Big Compliance Challenge, New Costs in FINRA Stress Tests" (September 30, 2015), http://blogs.reuters.com/financial-regulatory-forum/2015/09/30/broker-dealers-face-big-compliance-challenge-new-costs-in-finra-stress-tests/

36. Deloitte, "Quantum Dawn 2: A Simulation to Exercise Cyber Resilience and Crisis Management Capabilities" (October 21, 2013), http://www2.deloitte.com/us/en/pages/financial-services/articles/quantum-dawn-2-report.html

37. Deloitte, SIFMA, "Standing Together for Financial Industry Cyber Resilience: Quantum Dawn 3 After-Action Report (November 23, 2015), https://www.sifma.org/wp-content/uploads/2017/04/QuantumDawn-3-After-Action-Report.pdf

38. SIFMA (September 16, 2015), https://www.sifma.org/resources/general/cybersecurity-exercise-quantum-dawn-3/

39. New York State Department of Financial Services, "Cybersecurity Requirements for Financial Services Companies," 23 NYCRR 500 (February 15, 2017), http://www.dfs.ny.gov/legal/regulations/adoptions/dfsrf500txt.pdf

40. Ibid.

41. FINRA Series 99, Operations Professional Examination (OS) (January 21, 2018), http://www.finra.org/industry/series99

About the Companion Website

This book includes a companion website, which can be found at www
.wiley.com/go/capmarkets.com. Enter the password: swammy012.

Index

Advisory function, 62–63
Allocation, 119
Alternative trading systems (ATSs), 60
Anti-money laundering (AML), 60, 68–71
Anti-money laundering compliance officer (AMLCO), 68–69
Asset-liability management (ALM), 8, 11
Asset owners, types, 9–13
Assets under management (AuM), 31
Automated Conformation of Transactions (ACT), 73, 94

Bank for International Settlements (BIS), 47
Bank lending (substitution), capital markets (usage), 5–7
Bank loan/loan trading, 80
Bank loans, 119–120
Bank of Japan, 11
Bank-owned/affiliated broker-dealers, considerations, 114–115
Bankruptcy restructuring group, 81
Banks (investor type), 11
Barings Bank, fall, 130
Basel 2.5/3, 25–26
Basel Committee on Banking Supervision compliance guidelines, 50
    Corporate Governance Principles for Banks, 40, 42
    Principles for Sound Operational Risk Management, 37, 137
Basel Liquidity Coverage Ratio, rules, 11
Bayesian statistics/nets, 141
Board of directors
    board-level committees, core structure, 41–42
    makeup/mechanics, 39–43
Broker-dealers, 14
    net capital, 103t
Business activities
    monitoring/periodic testing, 63–64

reviews, 67–69
Business Continuity Management (BCM), 135, 137, 143
Businesses
    compliance officers, embedding, 76–77
    models, impact, 27–30
    transactions, surveillance, 64–66

Capital
    adequacy ratio, 6
    capital-raising activities, 79–80
    development, 9
    requirements, minimum, 102–105
    withdrawals, 107–108
Capitalization ratios, standards, 25–26
Capital markets
    compliance, 57
    development, 19–20
    environment, 2f
    functions, impact, 30–32
    products, 1–5
    stakeholders, 7–17
    substitutes, 5–7
Central banks (investor type), 11–12
Central counterparties (CCPs), 15, 27
Central Provident Fund, 10
Central securities depositories (CSDs), 15
Chain of command, 35
Chicago Mercantile Exchange (CME), 15
Chief compliance officer (CCO), 82–84
    obligations, 84
    roles/responsibilities, 59–61
Chief risk officer (CRO), 45, 46, 53
Chinese Walls, 61
Clapper, James R., 131
"Clear Desk Policy," 135
Clearinghouses, 15
Commissions, review, 95–96

Committee of Sponsoring Organizations of
the Treadway Commission (COSO)
Internal Control Integrated Framework,
37
Commodities, 4
Commodities Futures Trading Commission
(CFTC), 62, 72
Communication, importance, 49
Compensation, 52–54
Competitive landscape, change, 27, 30
Compliance, 50–51, 57, 132
  control room, 78–81
  coordination, 77
  culture, 75–76
  departments
    legal departments, differentiation,
      58–59
    roles/responsibilities, 61
  ethics, 77–78
  framework, cyber risk role, 129
  monitoring, 34
  officers
    embedding, 76–77
    reviews, 67
  organizational compliance/supervision,
    150–153
  program, effectiveness (assessment), 82–84
  registration department, 71–72
  regulatory examinations, 72–73
  regulatory inquiries, 73–75
  supervision, difference, 85–87
Compound annual growth rate (CAGR), 31
Comprehensive Capital Analysis and Review
  (CCAR), 114–115
Computer Security Incident Response Team
  (CSIRT), 137–138
Conduct Risk, 132
Consolidated supervised entities (CSEs), 106
Contracts for difference (CFDs), 10
Control Objectives for Information and
  related Technology (COBIT) (ISACA),
  140–142
Corporate values, setting/following, 35
Corporations (nonfinancial institutions), 7–8
Counterparty approvals, 93–94
Credit departments, 80
Credit risks, 126–128
Custodians, 15–16
Customer
  accounts, approval, 95
  complaints, 95

suitability, 95
Customer Protection Rule (SEA Rule
  15c3-3), 100, 115–122
  exemptions, 121–122
  possession/control, 115–117
  reserve formula, 117–121
CyberArk IV, 149
Cyber-awareness, 138
Cyber risk
  assessment, 136
  discipline, 151
  increase, 131
  insurance, 133
  measurement/assessment frameworks,
    139–144
  operational risk governance, relationship,
    129–136
  regulation, 144–150
  responsibilities, 151–152
  role, 129
  training instructional design, 135

Data Loss Prevention (DLP), 138
Data providers, 16–17
Death spiral, 121
Debt capital markets (DCMs), 13–14
DECIDE, 147
Defense model, 129–136
Defined contribution (DC), growth, 31
Department of Financial Services (DFS),
  Requirements for Financial Services
  Companies, 149–150
Depository Trust and Clearing Corporation
  (DTCC), 15, 104
Derivatives, 4–5
  sales departments, 80–81
Disclosure/reporting, 54
Distributed Denial of Service (DDoS),
  147, 148
Dodd-Frank Act Stress Test (DFAST)
  Baseline Scenario/Adverse Scenario,
    147
  schedules, filing, 146–147
Dodd-Frank Wall Street Reform and
  Consumer Protection Act, 25–27,
  46, 76–77, 146
Due diligence, 96

Early warning levels, reporting
  requirements/restrictions, 106–107

E-communications, surveillance
report/system, 65–66
Endowments/private foundations (investor
type), 12–13
Equities, 1, 3
Equity capital markets (ECMs), 13–14
European Central Bank, 11
European Union (EU), 34
Market Abuse Regulation, 46
Excess margin securities, 116
Exchanges, 15, 17–18
Exchange-traded funds (ETFs), 10, 32

Factor Analysis of Information Risk (FAIR),
143
Fails-to-receive/deliver, 120
Failure mode and effects analysis (FMEA),
141
Federal Deposit Insurance Corporation
(FDIC), 115
Federal National Mortgage Association
(FNMA), 9
Federal Reserve, 11
Board Regulation W, 34
Ferris, Baker, Watts, Inc. (FBW), 87
Finance
preparation/reporting requirements,
122–123
role, 99
Financial and Operational Combined
Uniform Single (FOCUS) Report,
122–123
Financial and Operations Principal, 91
Financial corporations, 8
Financial Crimes Enforcement Network
(FinCEN), 70
Financial Crisis (2008), 17, 45, 53
impact, 23
post-mortem, 112
regulatory reforms, 34–35
Financial Industry Regulatory Authority
(FINRA), 60–67, 72–75, 108
Central Registration Depository (CRD),
150–151
linkages, identification, 145–146
objectives, 144–145
Report on Cybersecurity Practices, 145
responsibilities, 134
trade execution, 94
Financial intermediaries, 7, 13–16

Financial Services Information Sharing and
Analysis Center (FS-ISAC), 148
Financial Services Sector Coordinating
Council (FSSCC), 147
Financial Stability Board (FSB), *Principles
for Sound Compensation Practices,* 53
Firm, trading strategy (understanding), 93
Fixed Income Clearing Corporation (FICC),
104
Fixed income securities, 3–4
Foreign Corrupt Practices Act (1977), 42, 77
Foreign exchange (FX), 4
Forwards, 5
Framework for Improving Critical
Infrastructure Cybersecurity Version 1.0
(NIST), 139–140
Free credits, 117–118
Freund, Jack, 143
Fully introduced agreement, 103
Funding risk, absence, 25
Futures, 5
Futures Commission Merchant (FCM), 105

Generally Accepted Accounting Standards,
101
General Securities Principal, 91
General Securities Sales Supervisor, 91
Global custodians, 16
Governance, 33, 36–48
committee approval, 96
model, cyber risk role, 129
Governments (investor type), 11
Government-sponsored entity (GSE), 9
Great Depression, government interventions,
112

Haircuts, 112–113
Haldane, Andrew, 130
Head supervisor, 89
Hedge funds, 12
Hidden leverage, 24

ICE Clear, 15
Identity and Access Management (I&AM),
145
Incident report, 70
Individuals (investor type), 10
Information providers, support, 7, 16–17
Information Risk Management (IRM), 130,
132, 135

Information Security Departments (ISDs), 131–132
"Information Security Governance" (ISACA), 139
Information Technology Laboratory (ITL), 139
Information technology (IT) personnel, impact, 74
Infrastructure
    project development, 9
    support, 7, 16–17
Initial public offering (IPO), usage, 3
Institutional trading area, exchange, 148–149
Insurers (investor type), 10
Interest rate swaps (IRSs), 5
Internal audit, 51–52
Internal controls, system, 46
Investment leverage, 8
Investment opportunities, breadth/depth, 20
Investors
    base, breadth/depth, 20
    types, 9–13
Issuers, 7–9

Jones, Jack, 143

Key performance indicators (KPIs), 138
Key risk indicators (KRIs), 138

Leverage
    investment leverage, 8
    ratio, 6
Liquidity coverage ratio (LCR), 6, 26, 114
Liquidity crisis, anatomy, 110–111
Liquidity risk
    absence, 25
    Net Capital Rule, relationship, 108–115
    reserve formula, relationship, 121
Loan-to-deposit ratio, 6
Long/short positions, 120
Long-term capital, 8
Loss data collection/analysis, 137

Malus/forfeiture provisions, 53–54
Market infrastructure (MI), 31
Markets
    infrastructure/regulations/supervision, strength, 20

risk, 126–128
    types, 17–19
Markup/markdown, review, 95–96
Material non-public information (MNPI), 61, 75, 78–81
Mergers and acquisitions (M&As), 14
    businesses, 79
MF Global, 113–114
MiFID, 14, 25–27
Moment-for-moment basis/compliance, 105
Monetary Authority of Singapore (MAS), 149
Monte Carlo simulation, 141
Municipal Securities Principal, 91
Municipal Securities Rulemaking Board (MSRB), 63–64
    Rule G-37, 78
Mutual funds, 12

NASDAQ, 73, 94
National Futures Association (NFA), 62
National Institute of Standards and Technology (NIST) Special Publications (SPs), 139
National Securities Clearing Corporation (NSCC), 104
Net asset value (NAV) computation, 130
Net capital
    computation, 101–102, 123
    requirement, 101
    computation method, 105t
Net Capital Rule (SEA Rule 15c3-1), 100–108
    liquidity risk, relationship, 108–115
New York Stock Exchange (NYSE), 62, 64, 76
Non-allowable assets, 101
Non-capital expenditures, 9
Norwich University Applied Research Institute (NUARI), 147

Off-balance-sheet (OBS), 123
Office of the Comptroller of the Currency (OCC), 111
Omnibus agreement, 103–104
Open Web Applications Security Project (OWASP), 146
Operational risk, 123–126, 130
    broker-dealer management, 124–125

governance, cyber risk, relationship, 129–136
processes, cyber risk integration, 136–138
Operational Risk Management, 130
Operations
cost, increase, 27, 29–30
preparation/reporting requirements, 122–123
role, 9
Operations Professional Examination, 91
Options, 5
Options Clearing Corporation (OCC), 104, 146
Order Audit Trail System (OATS), 73
Order management systems (OMSs), 64–65
Order/trade processing system providers, 16
Organizational compliance/supervision, 150–153
Oversight/control, 36–48
Over-the-counter (OTC) markets, 16, 18–19

Payment Card Industry (PCI) Data Security Standard (DSS), 145
Pension funds (investor type), 10–11
Personally identifiable information (PII), 145, 148
Primary markets, 17–18
Private equity funds, 12–13
Product approvals, 93–94
Public
communication, 95, 96
finance, 81
public-side businesses, 79
Public Company Accounting Reform and Investor Protection Act (Sarbanes-Oxley), 42, 144

Qualified securities, 118
Quantitative easing (QE), 11
Quantum Dawn (QD), 147–149

Ratings agencies, 17
Ready market, usage, 102
Reasonably expected near-term demand (RENTD), 77
Red Flags Rule, 145
Registered Options Principal Examination, 90
Registered representatives (RRs), 150–152
Regulations, overview, 24–27

Regulatory/supervisory framework, 20–21
Repurchase agreements (repos), 11–12, 28, 113
Research departments, 81
Reserve formula, 117–121
liquidity risk, relationship, 121
Restructuring groups, 81
Return on investment (ROI), 7
Revenue-earning capacity, reduction, 27–29
Reverse-repo financing, 28
Risk
appetite statement, 36
assessment frameworks (NIST/ISO/ISACA), 142–144
assessment governance/guidance (NIST/ISO/ISACA), 141–152
awareness, promotion, 35
governance framework, 37
identification/measurement, 46
management, role, 44–48, 132
risk-taking activities, monitoring/surveillance, 44
Risk Control Self-Assessment (RCSA), 136–137
Risk Self-Assessment (RSA), 136–137
Risk-weighted assets (RWAs), 26, 29
Root-cause analysis (RCA), 137–138, 141
Rule making, potential, 112–114

Sales supervisor, obligations, 95–96
SANS Institute, 146
Sarbanes-Oxley Act of 2002, 42, 144
Scenario analysis, 141
Secondary markets, 17–18
Secure coding, usage, 138
Securities
borrowed/loaned, 120
licensing, 92–93, 95, 96
syndicate activities, 79–80
Securities Act of 1933, 66, 92
Securities and Exchange Commission (SEC), 62, 72, 100
SEC-regulated broker-dealers, 85
Securities Industry and Financial Markets Association (SIFMA), 147–149
Securities Investor Protection Act, 115
Securities Investor Protection Corporation (SIPC), 115
Segregation of duties (SoD), 130, 134

Self-clearing, 104
Self-liquidation principle, 101
Self-regulatory organizations (SROs), 60, 100, 107, 144
Senior management
  oversight, 38–39
  role, 43–44
Short-term capital, 8
SIMEX, 130
Simon, Herbert, 135
Society for Worldwide Interbank Financial Telecommunication (SWIFT), 131
Sovereigns/governments, capital market usage, 9
Sovereign wealth funds (SWFs), 11
Standard Settlement Instruction (SSI), 152
Sub-custodians, 16
Superannuation, 10
Supervision, 89
  compliance, difference, 85–87
  delegation/escalation, 92
  organizational compliance/supervision, 150–153
  structure, 89–91
Supervisors, responsibilities, 92–96
Supervisory procedure template, 97
Suspense items, 120
Swap execution facilities (SEFs), 27
Swaps, 5
System development lifecycle (SDLC), 136

Technology risk, 130
Technology risk controllers (TRCs), 133–136, 147
Technology risk liaisons (TRLs), 133
Ted Urban, case study, 87
Tentative net capital, 101
Three Lines of Defense model, 132
TRACE, 32, 66, 94
Trade execution/pricing, review, 93
Trade reporting, 94
Trade repositories, 17
Trading
  activities, transactional review, 93
  limits approval, 93–94
  supervisor, obligations, 92–94
Training, core compliance functions, 66

U.S. Corporate Sentencing Guidelines, 34–35
User-access reviews, 138

Venture capital (VC) funds, 13
Volcker Rule, 14, 26, 76–77
Vulnerability management (VM), 138

Watts, Duncan, 129
Wollman, Bill, 146
Workplace pensions, 10
Worldwide Threat Assessment, 131
Written supervisory procedures, 97